Crafty Game Writing

Every writer dreams of creating their own game world and telling their own stories. But creating a new game from scratch is different from working on an established franchise. If you're writing for *Star Wars* or *Assassin's Creed* or the Marvel Universe, the groundwork has already been laid for you. But what if you are the person who has to lay that groundwork? Where do you start? How do you decide which, among the endless story options, is the right one? How do you create a story that plays nice with the gameplay and pulls the player in?

Alex Epstein, an experienced narrative director who has worked on half a dozen new IPs, takes you step by step through the process of creating compelling new worlds and characters that feel real.

Of course, many challenges are the same, whether you're creating your own game or working within a franchise. How do you make players think they have maximum freedom when they absolutely do not? What makes players inhabit a game story, not just skip past it? How can "dirty narrative" (a term Epstein coined) increase player engagement?

Packed with practical tips, *Crafty Game Writing: Secrets of Great Videogame Narrative* will help you understand the invisible infrastructure of player-pulled storytelling for video games – whether you aspire to make your own indie game or create the Next Big Thing for a AAA studio.

Features:

- This book is packed with tools to help the writer not only know what to write, but also how to write it well.
- The author has created the narrative for half a dozen entirely new games (not based on prior IP) and discusses how to build characters and worlds out of nothing. (Note: most video game writers, including game writing book writers, have worked in franchises.)
- This book includes the semi-heretical "dirty narrative" writing technique, using mysteries, absences, and translucent liars to pull the player into engagement with the game world and story.

Alex Epstein has created new video game worlds and characters for both AAA studios and indies. As a narrative director and lead writer for more than a decade, he has been crystallizing tips and tricks for the writers he has coached. That's this book.

His other books include *Crafty Screenwriting: Writing Movies That Get Made* and *Crafty TV Writing: Thinking Inside the Box.*

Crafty Game Writing
Secrets of Great Videogame Narrative

Alex Epstein

Illustrations by Marko Deška

CRC Press
Taylor & Francis Group
Boca Raton London New York

CRC Press is an imprint of the
Taylor & Francis Group, an **informa** business

Designed cover image: Jonathan Pennell

First edition published 2025
by CRC Press
2385 NW Executive Center Drive, Suite 320, Boca Raton FL 33431

and by CRC Press
4 Park Square, Milton Park, Abingdon, Oxon, OX14 4RN

CRC Press is an imprint of Taylor & Francis Group, LLC

Library of Congress Cataloging-in-Publication Data
Names: Epstein, Alex, author.
Title: Crafty game writing: secrets of great videogame narrative / Alex Epstein.
Other titles: Secrets of great videogame narrative
Description: First edition. | Boca Raton, FL: CRC Press, 2025. |
Includes bibliographical references and index. |
Identifiers: LCCN 2024054576 (print) | LCCN 2024054577 (ebook) |
ISBN 9781032963150 (pbk) | ISBN 9781032963242 (hbk) | ISBN 9781003589068 (ebk)
Subjects: LCSH: Video games—Authorship—Vocational guidance.
Classification: LCC GV1469.34.A97 E67 2025 (print) | LCC GV1469.34.A97
(ebook) | DDC 794.8—dc23/eng/20240108
LC record available at https://lccn.loc.gov/2024054576
LC ebook record available at https://lccn.loc.gov/2024054577

ISBN: 9781032963242 (hbk)
ISBN: 9781032963150 (pbk)
ISBN: 9781003589068 (ebk)

DOI: 10.1201/9781003589068

Typeset in Minion
by codeMantra

Contents

Acknowledgments

This book would not have come into the world without the help of a slew of people:

My writing and life partner, Lisa Hunter, without whom I would be a quarter of the writer I am.

Guillaume Provost, who invited me to write my first game, *Contrast*, based on little more than a funny movie I co-wrote; and in whose company I spent more than a decade with unparalleled creative freedom.

Atul Nath Mehra, Maxime Grégoire, José Aguirre, and Chris Chancey, who hired me to write games for them, too.

My friends Richard Dansky and Anna Megill, who invited me into their far-flung writer communities, without whom this path would be so much lonelier.

My friend Richard Rouse III, for much wise advice and insights about types of narrative.

Folks who kindly let me interview them: Jon Ingold, Lucien Soulban, Kelsey Beachum, Rhianna Pratchett, Kim Macaskill, Mikko Rautalahti, on my blog Complications Ensue, and, at MIGS, Warren Spector.

The folks who read this manuscript and gave me incisive notes, including Harmke Heezen, and my co-workers, Alexia Diane Fedail and Chantel Mitton.

Betsy Amster, who sold my screenwriting books and nagged me to write one about games.

Marko Dješka, who made the lovely cartoons. My editors at CRC Press, Sean Connelly and Alyss Barrazza, who were kind enough to suppose that folks might want to know what I think I know. And Toiya Kristen Finley, who introduced me to them!

Introduction: Games Are Fun

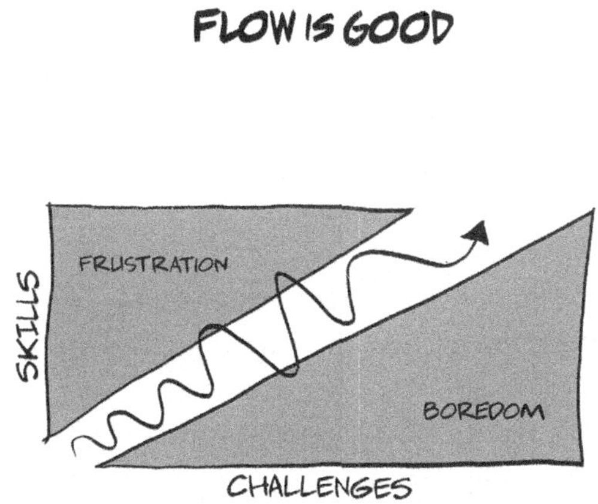

FIGURE 0.1 Flow is good.

Games are fun when the player is challenged enough that they are never bored, but not so much that they become frustrated. This is called "flow." In a flow state, the player can focus on a game for hours, tuning out the world and forgetting their troubles.

Any game, including narrative-driven games, should create a feeling of flow.

But a great narrative game can also take the player through emotional experiences. Like a great novel or movie or TV show, it might show the player what it's like to live through something the player has never experienced. Or it might take the player through an experience like the one they've lived through, enabling them to see events they've suffered from an outsider's perspective, and not feel so alone. A great narrative game can provide catharsis.

Papo & Yo shows the player what it's like to be in a relationship with an alcoholic, though it never mentions alcohol. *Papers, Please* puts the player in the shoes of an overworked bureaucrat who must choose between his humanity and his own family's needs. *God of War* is about a father's difficulty acknowledging that his son is becoming a man. *The Last of Us* is about a father's fear of letting himself care for a teenage girl because he's haunted by the death of his teenage daughter years ago.

Even without big emotions, narratives add meaning to gameplay. Narrative creates worlds. It creates an imaginative framework that makes the player care about the actions they're taking.

Gameplay is about "what do I do?" What are the rules of this game? How do I win it?

But without narrative, that's all you get. You can put the player in a flow state, but that's all they're going to feel. If you want players to have feelings, you have to have narrative.

Game narrative is there to answer the question, "why do I care?" Game narratives are there to engage the player's emotions so that the game means something to them.

Stories make people care. Arguably, stories are *what* make people care. We have trouble grasping facts until we can put them into a story, which is why a good story will often convince people in spite of the facts.

Human beings are hard-wired to learn and use languages. Cognitive science has shown that there is an area of the brain, Broca's area that enables human beings to talk. If that part of the brain is damaged, the patient can't use language anymore.

I can't prove it, but I believe human beings are *hard-wired* to understand the world through stories.

Human beings love to make series of events into stories. This tendency to create stories out of random patterns was adaptive when there were occasionally tigers in the tall grass, but now is the basis for all sorts of cognitive fallacies, such as believing that the dice are "hot" and the sunk-cost fallacy.

Note that when I'm talking about "narrative," I don't necessarily mean that the game has a single coherent story. World building is part of the narrative. World building invests meaning in the environments and objects and characters the player interacts with.

For example, in the *Civilization* franchise, there is no story beyond what the player does in the game. But there is a world. The player picks one of many historical civilizations, represented by their greatest leader – Alexander the Great for the Greeks, Julius Caesar for the Romans, etc. Each civilization has its own special powers and special military units. But that's not why we're playing *historical* civilizations. The game could make up special powers and military units and give them to civilizations called the Flong, the Flip, and the Floop. We're playing historical civilizations because the player wants to *be* Alexander, or Montezuma, or Saladin; they want to imagine the Greeks taking over the world, or the Aztecs, or the Arabs.

In *Into the Breach,* the player orders giant machines to fight giant alien bugs in order to save the human race. It's a thin veneer on a game that has been described as "death chess." The mechanics of the game are almost the whole experience. But if the enemy were machines with the same powers, instead of giant alien bugs, and if we weren't fighting to save the human race, then we wouldn't care as much about winning, or feel triumphant when we win.

Game narrative is everything that answers "Why do I care?"

Of course, game narrative doesn't do anything by itself. It only comes to life when a player plays through it.

An important tenet of passive entertainment is, "Show, don't tell." It's almost always stronger to show someone going through an experience than to have someone tell the reader that someone went through an experience.

With games, it's "Do, don't show." A movie can show you someone going through stuff. In a game, you go through some stuff. As far as possible, events that are key to the story should happen in the game mechanics, through the player's agency. The player shouldn't feel they're watching someone else doing stuff. They should be doing all the important stuff.

Why?

I'll tell you. But first, a caveat:

A Caveat

This is a book about how I try to write games well. Hopefully, it is filled with useful mental tools that will help you write games well. However, it is not a book about The One True Way to write games. Games are not a mature medium like movies or TV. We all know what a movie is, and we're pretty sure what a TV show is. Consequently, a fellow can write a book or two about how to write them. I did – they're called *Crafty Screenwriting: Writing Movies That Get Made* and *Crafty TV Writing: Thinking Inside the Box.* Twenty years after I wrote them, they're still in print. I'm proud of that. But games? We're still arguing about what's a game and what's not.

So, this book is about "craftier" game writing. There is no one crafty way to write a game. There are just tools that come in handy. Game narrative is a lot of different things. It is all the dialog and cinematics in big AAA adventure games like *Uncharted.* It is the story of what you do in the game *Journey*, a game in which there are no words – plus the event that sets you off on your journey, plus the world you journey in. It is also the conversations you have with the leaders of other civilizations in the *Civilization* games, and it is the backstory of the world in a multiplayer game like *World of Warcraft.* It is the thin but shiny veneer of science fiction laid on top of the gameplay mechanics of *Into the Breach.* It is the heartbreaking theme of *Papo & Yo.*

Point is, game narrative is a lot of things. No video game writer has worked on every kind of game. I certainly have not. I have written several adventure games and written and supervised writers on several others. I have worked on an online hero shooter and written a visual novel. I have also played hundreds of video games, from deck-builders to AAA games to "toys" like SimCity that are arguably not even games. I have worked on teams of seven developers up to over a hundred developers. But there are entire genres of games I have neither played nor worked on.

Video game narrative is harder than it looks, full of unobvious constraints, like the need to snooker the player into thinking they have maximum freedom when they absolutely do not. In return, video games offer a slew of techniques for delivering stories. Not just cinematics: games poach narrative delivery systems from comics, novels, interactive theater, radio plays, and text messaging. And of course, many of the best games allow the player to tell the story of the game through their choices in gameplay.

How do you write stories that stand out, that players will inhabit, rather than just observe? How do you write stories that the player will interact with? How do you take your writing to the next level?

I can't tell you how all games are written, because that doesn't exist, and I can't tell you how they're typically written, because that doesn't really exist either and might not even be useful. I can tell you how I write games and how to write games that I would like. And I think I can help you level up your writing.

Video game writing techniques are still being refined. Video game narrative has only existed since the 1980s, after all. It's still in its gangly adolescent phase. We're still figuring out all the ways to tell stories. We are still expanding the dramatic writer's tool kit. We are finding new subjects to explore. We are learning to give our heroes flaws and to let characters tell them lies and half-truths. We are discovering new ways in which our stories can go beyond linear narrative.

So, to get back to why the player character should always motivate the story in a video game:

CHAPTER 1

The Player

THE PLAYER IS THE HERO; THE HERO IS THE PLAYER

In a narrative video game, the hero is *you*, the player.

In film, TV, plays, and novels, the protagonist is a person distinct from themselves, who makes all his or her own choices, usually in some not-entirely-rational way that defines them as a memorable character. In fact, the central character is defined by those less-than-ideal choices they make for themselves. Their foolish, but human, choices make them naive (King Lear), or ambitious (Macbeth), or cocky (most of Tom Cruise's characters), or selfish (Larry David in *Curb Your Enthusiasm*), or miserly (Scrooge), etc.

We sometimes say that the reader "identifies with" the protagonist of a play, novel, movie, or TV episode. We mean that the reader or viewer sees something of themselves in the protagonist and can imagine themselves in the hero's shoes.

It's not fair to say that the reader of a novel or viewer of a TV episode is wholly passive. The reader does the work of imagining a whole world based on the words they read; the playgoer transports themselves to an imaginary world based on painted scrims. Even a TV or film viewer decides how they feel about the hero's choices. But these media are passive in the sense that the reader or viewer can't make choices for the hero.

In a video game, the player is active. They make at least some choices for the hero. Even in a "walking simulator," where the player just walks around and looks at stuff, the player decides where to walk and what to look at.

DOI: 10.1201/9781003589068-1

So, when we say the player "identifies" with the protagonist in games, we mean something more powerful than in other media. We mean they are participating in the story being told. The more the player gets to make choices for the player character, the more they, in a sense, *are* the player character.

That's what gives a video game its emotional power. Potentially, a video game can give a player a more powerful experience than passive entertainment, because *they* are the person navigating the world inside the computer.

As Richard Dansky says,

> There is a player shaped hole in the center of every videogame story. And as creators, we write to the possibility space of what the player might do. We don't dictate every moment. We prepare for the eventuality of what the player might choose to do at any given moment.

In 2K Games's *Bioshock*, that was *me* choosing to save the Little Sisters. So when they rescued me in the final boss battle, I felt vindicated in a way I would not have if I had only seen my player character, Jack, make that choice.

In Yager's *Spec Ops: The Line*, that was *me* choosing to use white phosphorus, with terrible consequences that left me feeling a bit sick, honestly.

In Ubisoft's *Far Cry 3*, that was *me* blasting everything with a flamethrower, and realizing that I, Jason Brody, was leaving behind the naive tourist kid I used to be, and becoming a bit of a monster.

As Ajay Ghale in Ubisoft's *Far Cry 4*, I had to choose which of two evil rebels I would support against the tyrant Pagan Min, making me complicit in whatever the kingdom turned into when we won.

As Arthur in Compulsion Games' *We Happy Few*, when I discovered that I was a heinous person, *I* had to make a choice between terrible self-knowledge or happy oblivion.

Potentially, detective games can be more immersive than detective novels. Even in the best detective novel, the reader doesn't have to solve the mystery. They just have to watch the detective solve the mystery. In a detective game such as Team Bondi/Rockstar's *LA Noire* or Lucas Pope's *Return of the Obra Dinn*, they have to solve the mystery or they don't win the game.

Practically, game narratives are rarely as powerful as the best examples in other media. That's usually because the narrative is rarely well integrated into the gameplay. A game narrative may just be a series of conversations (often cinematics) that play between stretches of gameplay. The player can only make choices about the gameplay; they can't decide what their player character does in a story. Essentially, the story is a movie punctuated by long stretches of gameplay.

But even with that structure, even when the story unfolds the same way in each playthrough, the fact that the player was playing the main character moments before the game made all the narrative choices for them, gives the player a feeling that *they* made those choices.

As Joel, in Naughty Dog's *The Last of Us*, I made a terrifying decision that affected the human race. Didn't feel too good about that.

As John Marston in Rockstar's *Red Dead Redemption*, I walked into a fusillade in order to buy time for my son to escape. Felt proud of myself.

As Wander in Sony/Team Ico's *Shadow of the Colossus*, I killed off the colossi, with awful consequences. Felt guilty, and sick at heart.

These three examples have issues, though. In *The Last of Us*, the game forces the player character to make a choice that the player probably would not make. In *Shadow of the Colossus*, it isn't until the end of the game that the player learns what the consequences of murdering the colossi are. They seem pretty monstrous. We're supposed to kill monsters, aren't we? Some players feel a bit railroaded by the way the plots turn out in these games. These endings drive a wedge between player and player character, possibly leaving the players feeling alienated. They're being punished for a moral choice they didn't actually get to make.

In *Far Cry 4*, the player does get to choose whether to give victory to the drug lord or the fanatic, but there is no option to bring peace and freedom to the mountain kingdom of Kyrat. The only way not to do evil is to stop playing the game. In *Far Cry 2*, you have to kill a dog in order to progress.

They're games, right? Shouldn't we get to make Joel's decision for him?

In those cases, I think, the writers weren't going for the most emotionally *intense* moment. They had a story they wanted to tell. They were more concerned with *what* the player would feel than *how much* the player would feel. Giving the player the key choice might have given the player a closer attachment to the player character. But the writers couldn't have told the story they wanted to tell if the player was allowed to opt out of it.

THE HERO MOVES THE STORY ALONG

Whether or not the player makes story choices, for the story to be satisfying, it must be driven by the main character. That means the story happens because of things they do, and is resolved by something they do. If the resolution occurs without the hero being central, we call that *deus ex machina*.

Very little should happen that the hero does not motivate in some way. If an enemy shows up, it is because the hero has become a threat to them. If the hero gets a new weapon, it is because they went on a quest, or killed an enemy, or crafted it. If someone comes to rescue the hero, it is because earlier in the game the hero rescued them; or because they are the comrades the hero was intending to join up with; or because the hero asked them to help and they're only now showing up.

Likewise, the player should know what the hero knows, and not much more. In a movie, you can reveal that someone the hero is depending on is a traitor. The audience will experience suspense: will the hero discover the truth in time? In a game, the same trick would only create frustration. The player knows that the friend is an enemy; why won't the game let the player act on that knowledge? Likewise, if there is anything that the hero knows that will be important for the player to know, it must be revealed to the player before it becomes important. Otherwise, the player will, again, be frustrated.

The player being the player character also makes ambiguous endings problematic in games. A movie might get away with an ending where we're not sure if the hero dies at the end or not. (*Shane*.) But the player needs to know if he died or not. Did he sacrifice himself nobly? Or did he win? And he certainly *would* know if he died or not!

Ideally, we will allow the player character to move the story along solely through the game mechanics. If your story is about killing monsters, that's something a video game can let your hero do. The game can have verbs like "hit" and "shoot arrow" and "dodge." Games do physical actions pretty well.

Verbs are the actions the game allows the player to make. A racing game will have verbs like "accelerate" and "brake." A stealth game will have "crouch," "take cover," and "knock out." A platformer might have "grapple," "glide," "mantle," and "jump." A fighting game will have a lot of specific combat moves, like "punch," "charged punch," and "parry." **A game is defined by its verbs.**

But even in a standard, naturalistic AAA game, we can give the player only a small set of verbs. For example, we limit how much of the environment they can interact with. In a lot of games, the player character cannot break a glass window. In *God of War*, Kratos can pick up a giant tree and swing it at enemies, but in a forest, he cannot push his way through bushes. In *Mass Effect*, Capt. Shepherd can't climb over a chest-high wall.

We limit the player's actions to a small set of (usually) physical verbs.

If your story is about killing monsters in order to win the heart of your beloved, however, "win the heart of your beloved" may be too abstract and too exotic for a video game to handle.

(Not that it's never been done as a mechanic. *Fable*, for example, allows you to woo, and even marry, any random human character you happen to meet. And there are dating sims like *Boyfriend Dungeon* and a ton of others.)

So what do we do in the many cases where we can't resolve the story through the game mechanics? We're going to be resolving the story purely through narrative moments – in cinematics, for example, or through other narrative delivery systems.

THE ILLUSION OF PLAYER AGENCY

We've run up against a key conundrum in video game narrative. There is an inherent contradiction between storytelling and gameplay. Stories tell you what happens; the storyteller decides. In gameplay, the player wants to decide what to do. If you let players make all the choices, you can't tell a good story. If you don't let players *feel* like they're making choices, they feel railroaded.

We can't give them limitless choices, after all. Every consequential choice you give the player multiplies the amount of work it will take to finish the game. Every time the player chooses between this or that, they're going to miss all the content on the story branch they didn't pick.

So how do we square this circle? How do we give the player a feeling of limitless possibility and personal power, when their actions are actually quite limited?

This is one of the less obvious things that narrative does in a video game. The story can convince the player that the things we enable them to do are the only things they want to.

The player wants to feel like they can do anything. They want to feel like they're having an adventure; they want to feel in charge of the hero's destiny. When they are not actually in charge, because the story the game is telling has to make decisions for them, then the game narrative must create what Siobhan Aisling dubbed the **illusion of player agency**.[1]

If narrative makes us murder all the bad guys, and we get to murder them, then we don't feel like we're being forced to do it, even though we are being forced. We want to do it! If we are supposed to be chasing someone down a forest path, we don't feel bad that we can't peel off and go roaming through the underbrush.

The illusion of player agency is essential; breaking it can be fatal. If all I can do in gameplay is shoot people, and the game gives me a reason why I might want to talk to them, then I will become aware of just how limited my options are. If I find a gun in a combat game, and there is no way for me to pick it up and fire it, I am going to be frustrated.

So, it is critical to **align what the player wants to do and what the player character wants to do**. They don't have to want to do it *for the same reason* as the player does. They may have different reasons for doing whatever it is. But they need to want to go to the same places and do the same things.

FIGURE 1.1 Player motivation needs to align with player character emotion

In *God of War*, Kratos wants to take his wife's ashes to the top of the mountain. This objective doesn't mean much to the player at first. So, the game developers at Sony had to make sure that taking those ashes up that mountain requires exploring strange mystical planes of existence and killing a lot of trolls – which is what the player is here to do.

Then, as soon as possible, they had to earn the player's desire to get to the top of that mountain, by hinting that it is a mysterious goal whose resolution will be an exciting revelation. There is a mystery why Kratos' dying wife asked him to take her ashes up the mountain, and we can only resolve it by completing the quest.

There is a constant friction between level designers and story folk. For a level designer, the player character has an objective in order to push them in the direction of some fun gameplay. As far as the writer is concerned, though, the player character does not know they are in a video game. So, they need an in-world reason to want to do whatever level design wants the player to want to do. And it has to make sense for that character in that world to have that objective.

Friction isn't necessarily a bad thing. It keeps you warm, for one thing.

Aligning the player and player characters' goals can create difficulty because, to tell a good story, the writer may want the main character to do something that the player doesn't want to do.

The hero of a novel can do any rotten thing the story needs them to do. But the hero of a game *is* the player. If you make them do something they don't want to do or punish them for doing something you just asked them to do, the player may rebel, lose engagement, and possibly hurl their controller at the television. Expensive!

If the writers want the player character to do something the player doesn't normally want to do, they have to earn that decision.

So, to get back to *The Last of Us*: Neil Druckmann, the creative director, wanted to tell a story in which a man makes a shocking, essentially selfish choice that few players would choose to make. But it is earned. Everything that the player has done as either of the game's main characters has led up to this decision. Everything leading up to that awful final decision makes it plausible that Joel would make it; everything justifies that to the player. Few players would make that choice, but it makes sense that that character, in that situation, would.

The player may find the hero's choice objectively outrageous. But emotionally it is satisfying.

On the other hand, many players, including me, had problems with Ellie's and Abby's revenge quests in *The Last of Us 2*. If the player doesn't feel that the revenge is legitimate or important, they may find it hard to murder all the people the game puts in their way.

BAFTA-nominated narrative director Lucien Soulban:

> You really have to work to get the player on board with those motivations. You take a look at a game like *Watchdogs 1*. The main character was seeking vengeance. But we almost never saw the niece, we never got to know her, interact with her in a meaningful way, or say, fully saw what happened to her. That character was never a part of our experience. As a result, there was a disconnect. The motivation of the character was only that of the character's....
>
> Revenge has become a shorthand in a lot of games.... "Oh, people want revenge. It'll be fine. Somebody wronged you." And you can empathize that if it happened to your family, you'd want to do that as well. But it's a tricky line to walk. The player needs to feel that they've been brought into the situation, or it's just the character going off on their own, and the player feeling, "Well, OK, I guess.... I'll just use this as an excuse to perpetuate violence."[2]

In *Spec Ops: The Line*, the player has to commit an atrocity in order to progress. The story only reveals that it's an atrocity after you commit it. Many players hated being spanked for doing something the game required them to do. They felt they'd been railroaded into committing an atrocity.

On the other hand, Captain Martin Walker's awful decision fits into his story arc; and the story has to force you to do dreadful things because it wants you to feel more and more alienated from the main character. We are supposed to question Walker's objectives more and more as the story unrolls. The decision isn't necessarily earned at the point it happens, but it is definitely earned by the end of the game.

Perhaps the rule is, if you're going to force the player to make a lousy choice, it better be fundamental to the story – a key element of either the premise or the conclusion.

PLOT LOGIC AND LUDO-NARRATIVE DISSONANCE

The inverse is also true. If the player wants to do something, we need to make sure the player character has a plausible reason they want to do it, too.

In *We Happy Few*, we had a mission where our anti-hero, Arthur, needed to go looking for the delivery boy, Meat Boy. He finds out that Meat Boy is late. An objective pops up on the player's screen, telling them to find out why.

But why should Arthur go chasing off after a late delivery boy? When your Amazon delivery is late, you don't go looking for the truck. People are late every day. Unless they are late with your replacement kidney, it's just an annoyance.

"Because it will send him on an adventure" is not a good reason. Arthur doesn't know he's in a video game. Arthur has had a lot of adventures lately. Too many, really, and he'd just as soon not have another.

It's important to do a reality check on the player character's situation. What would make them go off on this particular adventure?

Hmmm. Maybe the delivery boy is never late. Okay, that's a start. That makes it more worrisome. But still, why should Arthur be perturbed?

Our creative director, David, suggested, "Maybe he knows him."

Ah! Of course. The delivery boy was the only real friend of our hero's brother Percy. Arthur's whole journey has been about trying to reach Percy so he can make sure he's okay, something Arthur has spectacularly failed to do in the previous 20 years. Making sure that Meat Boy is okay is a way Arthur can feel he's doing something for Percy.

Now the mission is personal. Note that the level design has not changed at all, only the meaning of the quest. That changed meaning in turn gave us an emotionally powerful way to resolve the mission.

Design sometimes crashes into the narrative. It is sometimes frustrating to have to find ways to legitimize a level design that disregards the situation of the player character. But if you dig deep, you can often find out new things about your imaginary world.

SIDE QUESTS

Plot logic can become an issue with side quests. If the main character has an urgent main objective – finding his missing daughter, escaping a nightmarish city, investigating a murder, stopping machines from massacring all intelligent life in the galaxy – then why would they put that objective on hold to do something else?

Sure, it is fun for the player, and maybe the player is tired of the main plot at the moment. But why would the hero put their urgent objective on hold?

We might need to make clear that the player character is more likely to defeat the Big Bad if they do a bucket of side quests and win experience and find gear or assure the loyalty of their allies. Or we could make clear that something in their wounded psyche is making them put an apparently less important objective first.

(As we'll discuss later, when a character needs to do something illogical, the fix is often to give them a strong, character-based irrational reason to do it.)

If we don't pay attention to plot logic, we end up with **ludo-narrative dissonance**, Clint Hocking's term[3] for when the story and gameplay contradict each other.

In *Black Ops: Splinter Cell*, you are leading a government team against terrorists who have a credible plan to murder everyone in Chicago. But the government doesn't give you the really good guns at first. You have to buy them with money you earn from missions. It makes sense for the gameplay loop, but it's nonsensical narratively. And that breaks immersion. Dude, what?

In *Baldur's Gate 3*, by the time you are into the third act, the clock is ticking and important characters are telling you that you must complete certain quests in a hurry or everyone you know will be doomed. But the game offers you a zillion fun side quests that have no impact on the doom clock.

In *Far Cry 3*, you are theoretically rescuing your friends, who are in grave danger, but the game offers lots of side quests. Lucien Soulban again:

> So in the main storyline, you're like, all my friends are kidnapped, everything is terrible. -- Oh, look, I can kill a rhinoceros to craft a bigger wallet! And while some people appreciated not having that pressure on them all the time, some players felt guilty for engaging in frivolous activities when their friends were being held hostage.

In *Fallout 4*, you are theoretically looking frantically for your kidnapped child. But the game encourages you to build yourself a sweet little settlement.

A fake doom clock is a familiar trope, to the point where if a game tells you that you must do a thing urgently, experienced players assume that means that you should do everything *except* deal with the urgent main story, because once you do the urgent thing, the game will move to a new state, and some or all of the side quests will disappear.

FIGURE 1.2 Don't be in such a hurry!

As a game writer, you will rarely get to cure these contradictions by altering the gameplay, unless you are at one of the rare narrative-driven studios where the development teams take gameplay, art, and narrative all into account as they are concepting the game. Instead, it will usually be the job of the narrative team to "take the curse off" the contradiction. Your job will be to surgically change the story so that the contradiction isn't there, or doesn't appear to be there, anymore.

NOTES

1 https://siobhanaisling.wordpress.com/2020/07/31/the-illusion-of-player-agency/.
2 Interview with author on author's blog, *Complications Ensue*, December 1, 2020.
3 https://clicknothing.typepad.com/click_nothing/2007/10/ludonarrative-d.html.

CHAPTER 2

Story

WHAT IS STORY?

A story is:

- A character
- who wants something but
- can't get it,
- until the outcome, when they get it, or don't.

A *good* story is:

- A character we care about
- who has a relatable problem or opportunity
- who faces obstacles, an opponent, and/or their own personal flaw
- who has something to lose (jeopardy)
- and something to gain (stakes).

A good potboiler novel has these five elements, a good movie script has them, an effective play has them, and a good video game story has them.

DOI: 10.1201/9781003589068-2

A Character We Care About

We need to care about what happens to the main character. We don't need to *like* them, necessarily. We just have to care how things turn out for them.

It's nice if the player likes the main character. But it's not necessary. The reader or the audience doesn't like Frankenstein or his creature, but they care what happens to them. I don't like Arthur Morgan in *Red Dead Redemption 2*, Alan Wake in *Alan Wake*, or Franklin Clinton in *Grand Theft Auto V*. But I care what happens to them.

To some extent, we automatically care about the main characters because we are playing them. And many amazing video games go no further than that. They have blank slate characters. The Messenger in *Fallout:*

FIGURE 2.1 First person hands.

New Vegas is a cipher. The investigator in *Obra Dinn* is an empty shell. And so on.

However, these games do not create as emotional an experience as a game that tells a story with a main character. They are fun, they create flow, but the player is not really living a story. They don't come to care about the main character except as a sort of narrative glove to put their hand into.

Jon Ingold, Narrative Director of *Heaven's Vault*:

> I've got very little interest in blank characters for the player to project onto. I find it makes for very disposable storytelling. We did it for Sorcery! and it worked out ok, I think, but it does reduce every encounter to "let's meet another funny local!" For me, character comes first, and story comes second. I think people are interested in human beings, and what those humans do is only a vehicle for letting us spend time with them.[1]

I enjoyed *Fallout: New Vegas.* I loved exploring the world, and combat was engaging. I went around exploring a unique, imaginative, immersive world, talking to some people and shooting some others in the face. But I did not have an emotional experience. The player character is a blank. The player doesn't see them. They don't have a name. They don't have a voice.

Same for Link in *Zelda: Breath of the Wild* or *Tears of the Kingdom*, or any other Zelda game. He is the only one who can save Hyrule, but as a character, he barely exists. Same for Gordon Freeman in the *Half-Life* games. There is no doubt those are super-fun, super-successful games. But very few players are moved to tears by Link's story.

It is common for first-person games, where you see the world as if through the main character's eyes, to have a blank main character. Lucien Soulban:

> In Ubisoft FPS's, we made a conscious decision never to pull the camera out of the character's head.... The character is a tabula rasa, because [Ubisoft HQ in] Paris, and Editorial, wanted you to feel like the real "you" is dropped into the game world.[2]

It is relatively more common for main characters in third-person games, where you see the character you're playing on the screen, to have personalities – though some third-person main characters are almost equally blank.

It is possible for *other* characters to create an emotional experience for the player. Like a lot of people, I was sad when I had to throw the Companion Cube into the fire in *Portal*, and that was just a cube with a heart painted on it. I'd lugged it around for a while, so I didn't want to throw it in an incinerator. But what is emotional is the story of that cube, not my player character's story. My player character, Chell, is trying to escape a hellish testing center, but I am never involved in them emotionally.

Of course, giving the player character a personality, while allowing drama and catharsis, creates another conundrum. We want the player to feel like they *are* the player character. But the more I know about the PC, the more I know that he or she is not me. I automatically care about me, but what makes us care about *them*?

Flaws

A typical video game hero has no flaws. Link has nothing distinctively wrong with him, aside from an awkward tendency to go into random villagers' houses and smash their pots. Jesse in *Control* has no weaknesses, though her brother clearly has some issues. Morgan Yu in *Prey* has a backstory and a lot of abilities, but I couldn't tell you why you might or might not want to have him over for dinner.

Geralt in *The Witcher* lives in a world full of living, breathing characters with very human flaws – the annoying Dandelion, the conflicted Bloody Baron, and wily Dijkstra. Geralt has distinctive drives – he wants to be with Yennefer and protect Ciri. He has a code that defines who he will and won't kill for money. But the only flaw you could name is that he's a cold fish.

The problem with player characters not having flaws is, *we don't care about fictional people because of their virtues; we care about them because of their flaws.* Flaws are what make them human; flaws are what grounds them in our own experiences with other humans.

We don't care about Han Solo because he's a good pilot; we care about him because he's a jerk. Ellie and Joel in *The Last of Us* are both people who would be hard to love in real life, but we can relate to their flaws. We know people like that, or we are like that, so we care what happens to them.

Point of View

If we have a main character, then for maximum emotional engagement we need to stick closely to their point of view. If something's important, and the main character knows it, the players need to know it right away.

Let me qualify that a bit: we need to stick closely to their *emotional* point of view. That's not literally what they're experiencing when they're experiencing it. It includes things that happen that the player character only finds out about later. But it excludes things they never find out about, and it excludes things that don't affect or concern the main character.

Naturally, the player character knows lots of things the player doesn't. But if they know something important and relevant, we better fill the player in long before the player needs to know it. (That's sometimes called "laying pipe.")

The player character absolutely must drive the narrative. There are no Ishmaels in video games, taken along for the boat ride. Whatever happens in the story should come about because of who the main character is and what they do. If we learn the answer to a mystery, it should be because the player went looking for that answer. If a monster attacks, it's because the player character did something to provoke it.

A Relatable Objective

This character that we care about needs a problem or opportunity that gives them a goal.

Video games are usually pretty good at setting up clear objectives. After all, games have win conditions. If you can't win, it's not a game. (That's why the makers of *The Sims* consider it a "toy," not a game.)

Objectives should be relatable: save the princess, find your brother, stop the terrorists, get vengeance on the guys who shot you, escape the testing center, and fight off the alien invasion.

If it is not immediately relatable, then the story needs to convince the player to care about it by showing what it means to the main character.

Obstacles, an Opponent, and a Personal Flaw

A game story presents challenges to the player character. The challenges define the genre of the game. Where the obstacles make traversal challenging, the game can be considered a **platformer**. Where there are opponents trying to shoot him, and he can shoot them, we're playing a **shoot'em up** (a "schmup").

Often the hero has a special talent for opposing these challenges. In *Red Dead Redemption*, the hero, John Marston, is a superlative gunslinger. In *Tomb Raider*, Lara Croft is exceptional at climbing, as well as being a superb archer. Mario is quite a jumper. Wahoo!

It's often good if the enemies reflect the hero in some way.

- The enemy may represent the hero's deepest fear.
- They may be someone who has hurt the hero, or those he loves, in the past; defeating them is vengeance.
- It may be that the enemy represents the opposite of what the hero represents. If the hero is an idealist, their enemy is a materialist. If the hero stands for freedom, the enemy stands for dictatorship. This philosophical difference is often the theme of the story.

It is good if the hero has a personal flaw that makes it particularly hard for them to win out. In theater, Hamlet is too thoughtful: he investigates when he should take action.[3] Othello is too rash: he takes action when he should investigate.

Likewise, in *Spec Ops: The Line*, Martin Walker desperately wants to be a hero because of his past failures. That prevents him from seeing the truth of what is going on. In *We Happy Few*, both Arthur and Ollie have done terrible things and lied to themselves about it. Finding out the truth is particularly difficult for them because they don't really want to know it. As General Byng reminds Ollie, "the easiest secret to keep is one nobody wants to know."

Flawed heroes, and particularly heroes whose flaws get in the way of their objectives, are rare in video games, so far. But they are a good way to intensify the story.

Drama is the struggle of someone to get something they want when they are opposed by something in their way, whether it's an enemy, an obstacle, or their own inner conflict. This struggle should seesaw. It should reach extremes. There need to be moments where it looks like the hero can achieve their goal and moments where it looks all but impossible.

I like to think there's a math to dramatic struggle. If the hero is going to end up succeeding, then there needs to be a moment where it looks like all is lost. (This moment is often about three-quarters through the story – what we'd call the end of the second act in traditional movie screenplay structure.) If the hero is going to lose – well, hah, video game stories almost by definition require success at the end, because if it's a game, it needs a win condition. But if one day a hero *was* going to lose, then there needs to be a moment when it looks like they are going to win.

The harder the opposition in the struggle, the stronger the drama is. If the hero has a flaw, it should be a big flaw that threatens to destroy them. If they have an enemy, it should be a powerful enemy. If they have a distance to travel, it must be a very hard road, often straight up a mountain.

Think about a romance story, whether it's a romance or a straight-up five-hanky weepie. Unless there is an external obstacle (Romeo & Juliet), the internal obstacles need to be big. That's why rom-coms often start with the future lovers disliking each other. It gives more room for them to travel to their realization that they're perfect for each other. Same goes for buddy comedies, which are all about how unfit the buddies are for each other, until in the end they pull out the unlikeliest of victories.

If your hero has an internal flaw, it should be a flaw that multiplies the difficulty for the hero of surmounting those obstacles and opposing those enemies.

You want the **narrative distance** the hero travels to be great. Anything you can do as a writer to increase the narrative distance that the hero travels is worth looking at.

Jeopardy

Jeopardy is tricky in video games. Theoretically, the jeopardy for most player characters is death. In any combat game, the enemy can kill you. In many platformers, you can fall to your death.

But this is fake jeopardy. Sure, the hero can be killed. But the player knows that they will respawn at the last save point. Or, in a roguelike, they'll just play again. So, the player is not that scared of getting killed. Avoiding getting killed is part of the game's challenge. It is part of the fun. But it is not part of the story, unless getting killed and then respawning is part of the story, as in *Hades, The Outer Wilds*, or *Bioshock*. After all, if the hero is permanently dead, it is hard (though not impossible) to paint that as a win for them.

So how do we create a sense of jeopardy?

Some games have multiple endings. The jeopardy is in the "bad" ending. The hero will almost always survive to the end. But they may fail to achieve 100% of their goal. They may not save everyone they set out to save.

We can put non-player characters (NPCs) in danger. When the story threatens the life of someone that the player character and player care about, the player does not know if the NPC will survive. In many games, key NPCs die. That may be an emotionally powerful moment. It may come at the beginning, as in *Heavy Rain*, or at a critical point, as in *Mass Effect*. Or they may be threatened as part of the climax, as in *The Last of Us*.

Jeopardy can be personal or universal. Personal jeopardy is something bad happening to someone the hero cares about: a best friend, a mother, a son. Universal jeopardy is when something bad will happen to a large group: the nation, the continent, the human race, all sentient life in the galaxy. It's not bad to have jeopardy at both levels, but there must be personal jeopardy for us to care emotionally.

It is possible, of course, to kill off a main character, usually in the finale of a story. That's usually fairly shocking, and it needs to be carefully justified by the theme. For example, in *Red Dead Redemption*, the hero does everything he does in order to save his wife and son. Finally, he sacrifices his life for them.

Up to that point, we have learned a lot about what drives him. The only thing he really cares about is his family. So if he can save them by sacrificing himself, that's a win. In another game I worked on, the father was motivated by a desire to protect his son. The player isn't worried about him; he's the player character. We're worried his son may not make it. That's the personal jeopardy.

Stakes

Stakes are why the objective feels important. Why is important that the hero succeeds? What will I, the player, feel good about achieving?

As with jeopardy, stakes may be personal, or personal and universal. In movies, almost every Tom Cruise character wants to earn his dead father's approval (personal). He gets it by defeating his country's enemies (*Top Gun*, *Mission: Impossible*) or saving the human race (*Edge of Tomorrow*, *Oblivion*) (universal).

In the final DLC (downloadable content) for *We Happy Few: We All Fall Down*, Victoria Byng wants to do her duty so she can win her father's approval. But that turns out to be worthless when she realizes he's a coward. After that, she is struggling to earn her mother's approval. She does it by saving the entire town of Wellington Wells (universal), though at a terrible cost to herself.

In *Psychonauts 2*, Raz wants to prove he is worthy of being a "psychonaut" (personal). He does that by defeating Maligula, who wants to destroy the Psychonauts organization (universal).

In *Dishonored*, Corvo both wants to save the Empire from a coup (universal) and regain his honor (personal).

On the other hand, in *80 Days*, Passepartout wants to help his employer go around the world in 80 days. That's personal. There are no universal consequences. In *A Short Hike*, Claire simply wants to climb to the top of Hawk Peak so that she can get enough cell phone signal so her mother can call her. Edith Finch, in *What Remains of Edith Finch*, wants to understand what happened to the members of her family. That's entirely personal.

It is possible to have universal stakes with no personal stakes, but it's weaker. I can relate to Raz wanting to be a psychonaut – anyone who's really wanted a job doing something they care about can relate. I have no emotional attachment to the fictional Psychonauts organization.

The Ghost

It's not a requirement like the other five elements of the story, but the hero often has a "ghost," named for the ghost in *Hamlet*. At the beginning of that play, the ghost of Hamlet's father demands that Hamlet avenge his murder.

The ghost is whatever haunts the player character. What is the bad thing that happened to them before the beginning of the story, that leaves them with a psychic wound?

Often, an implicit part of the stakes of the story is the healing of this wound, the laying to rest of this ghost. Hamlet dies (sorry for the spoiler), but avenges his father.

In *The Last of Us*, Joel saves Ellie. That lays to rest the ghost of his own daughter, whom he failed to save long ago.

God of War begins with Kratos and his son Atreus building the funeral pyre for Kratos's wife, Atreus's mother. She is the ghost that drives both of them up the mountain. Discovering why she wanted her ashes scattered on top of the mountain lays that ghost to rest (more for Atreus than for Kratos, who isn't the type to mourn and move on).

Note that stakes may just be the reverse of the jeopardy. Jeopardy: catastrophe. Stakes: avoiding catastrophe. But they may be separate, and the hero may avoid jeopardy without achieving the stakes.

TELL YOUR STORY OUT LOUD

Say you're trying to come up with a story for a game or for a quest in a game. You have a general idea of what the story is about, but level design has not already designed the level.

There is an incredibly powerful tool for coming up with stories that are coherent and yet surprising. Almost no one uses it.

Tell your story out loud.

A funny thing happens when you tell a story out loud. It gets better. Each time you tell it out loud, without notes, it gets better.

You see that the person you're pitching your story to is getting bored, so you shorten something to get to the good bits faster. Or you make up something more fun.

Your listener is confused, so you focus things for them.

You can't remember what comes next, so you realize that there is no logical connection between two story beats.

You know how a story about something that happened to you gets better? Maybe you exaggerate a little more each time? Maybe you add embellishments? Maybe you just figured out how to tell it better? The same thing happens when you pitch a story off the top of your head – whether it is to fellow writers, or even better, gamers who are not writers.

This does *not* happen when you work on something on the page. Once you've written your story down, it is frozen. You can chip away at it, you can rewrite it, but it will not fix itself in the telling. If you read it, you will naturally skim the boring bits, rather than suffering from how boring they are. You won't have any trouble remembering what comes next, because there it is on the page, so you won't realize the story is missing some logic there.

It is *hard* to pitch a story live. It is awkward and a bit embarrassing. Most writers are introverts and don't like standing up and presenting things unless they have their whole presentation written down. People might laugh at you. They might start looking at their phones.

But if your story is working, you'll know it, because they're not looking at their phones, they're intent on you. What are you going to say next?

Don't write your story until you can tell the whole thing off the top of your head. At that point, you know that it's coherent and entertaining. It's a good story.

In most cases, you won't get to pitch anyone a game story. Even as a senior writer (or narrative director for that matter!) you will often come on to the project after other people have already built the overall story structure, or the level designers have already blocked out the level, and you are trying to flesh out a skeleton that is already there. But it's still worthwhile to hear how your story sounds on its own. Looking at the page, it's easy to get distracted by the multiple mandates you've been given and forget that the player does not care about the constraints you wrote under. Seriously, try this technique.

IT'S NEVER ONLY ABOUT THE MONKEYS

One day, my wife Lisa was rebreaking a story. The third act action sequence, involving some monkeys, was driving her crazy.

That evening I suggested she think about, "What is your hero's deepest fear? The action sequence is where she confronts and surmounts it." In the morning, she told me, "I've got the whole thing."

In a game, there will be a lot of action in the last act. However, in the story, the action should not only be about the hero (and player) achieving the external goal. They should also be doing something that resolves their emotional wound, that lays their ghost to rest, that surmounts their deepest trauma. As TV writer John Rogers writes, "Don't write action scenes. Write suspense scenes that require action to resolve."[4]

It's not about the monkeys. It's never about the monkeys. Well, not only the monkeys.

SURPRISE VS. INEVITABILITY

The outcome of a game story, like any story, should feel both surprising and inevitable.

Inevitable: the outcome should feel like the most satisfying way for the story to conclude. In retrospect, everything that happened during the story led up to this ending. This ending resolves the hero's unfinished business and lays his "ghost" to rest. Little bits of the story that seemed accidental or irrelevant turn out to be essential bits of the conclusion. In some way, the hero motivated all of the things that happened after the premise, and they turned out to be the only person who could have resolved things. If a loose end is left untied, that is because it is more satisfying if it is left loose.

So how can you achieve surprise in a story? If the story is well told, the seeds of the ending are in the beginning. The player probably can figure out what a satisfying ending will be. You can surprise them by not having a satisfying ending, but that is, well, unsatisfying. You can make surprise possible by not putting the seeds of the ending in the beginning, but then the ending won't be a satisfying payoff.

Either way, the player will want their money back. They will refund the game on Steam; they will trash it on social media.

So how is it possible to throw them off the scent?

Well, we don't know *how* the hero will succeed. We know that the hero will succeed. It's a game. We don't know how the ending will affect them emotionally, or how it will change them. We can't foresee how the rhythms or pacing of the game will switch up, and how events that we knew would probably happen, happened at times we did not think they would.

SCHMUCK-BAITING

We can, to an extent, ask the player to suspend their disbelief. We can use sleight-of-hand so that the player does not pay too much attention to the clues we have put in the story about how the story must end. That is, until the ending is upon them.

Like Agent Mulder in *The X-Files*, the player *wants* to believe.

Asking the player to believe something will happen that absolutely will not happen is sometimes called "schmuck-baiting." TV writer Jane Espenson:

> Sometimes, tricking the audience is good.... If you create a creepy and menacing atmosphere and you want your audience to expect a vampire attack, when instead you've got the vampires attacking somewhere else entirely, that might be called schmuck bait without any sense that the writer has done something inelegant ... in fact, they've done something very effective.
>
> Most writers, and most writers' rooms, however, use the term to refer to an attempt to fool the audience into thinking something is going to happen which any intelligent viewer KNOWS won't happen. If Alan Shore were on the verge of death in an episode [of Boston Legal], and you hadn't read anything in Entertainment Weekly about James Spader [the actor who plays him] getting fired, then you probably shouldn't be too worried about his survival.[5]

But if we want a surprise, then we need to give the player room to believe (to suspend their disbelief) that what obviously is going to happen may somehow not happen.

The secret to successful schmuck-baiting is to commit to it. If you want the player to believe that a character is going to die, then do all the narrative things you would do if that character was really going to die. Hit all the notes. Have them say things that will later sound like goodbye. Have them show us a picture of their wife and baby. Have them tell us about their dream to retire to a small village to make shoes. Give them something horrible that they've done, that only their death would redeem. All the things that would make their death dramatically satisfying, do those things.

If you shorthand any of that, then the player will sense that you are not really serious about killing off the character.

Consider: what are the game tropes you'd be tempted to use if you were really going in the direction that you are (surprise!) not going in? This is the perfect place to use all those clichés that you should never use normally.

Schmuck-baiting requires tracking the players' expectations and emotions. You should be doing that even when you're not schmuck-baiting. It is a key aspect of game narrative work to know how the player is feeling and what they think is going to happen next. You may want to subvert expectations, or you may want to fulfill them, but either way, you need to know what those expectations are.

DEUS EX MACHINA

As mentioned in Chapter One, the hero is supposed to motivate all the things that happen in the story, rather than have a plot device come out of nowhere to resolve problems the hero is facing. If Dorothy, in *The Wizard of Oz*, had not caused the Wicked Witch to melt by throwing water on her – if instead it had suddenly started raining, that would be *deus ex machina.*

Normally the solution to a *deus ex machina* plot device is to get rid of it and replace it with events that the player character has set in motion through their own actions. However, you may be stuck with the plot device because gameplay or level design has decided they like it, or because someone high up in the studio said something in an elevator to the narrative director.

In that case, come at it the other way. A *deus ex machina* comes out of nowhere, right? One thing that will help is to foreshadow the event. It can't come out of nowhere if we see it coming. If storm clouds have been gathering all day, and the characters have remarked on it, then rain will not feel like it came out of nowhere.

Then find ways for the player character to own the plot device. We are stuck with the rainstorm killing the witch. Is there a way that Dorothy can trigger the rainstorm, or at least trigger the witch getting caught in it?

Well, as a Kansas girl, she probably can't do much to make rain fall. But she could develop a plan to lure the witch out onto the balcony, knowing that a thunderstorm is brewing.

This is how Gandalf defeats the trolls in *The Hobbit.* Sunlight turns trolls into stone. A rising sun coming up unexpectedly might feel like a *deus ex machina.* But he keeps the trolls arguing all night so that they fail to notice the sun coming up. He owns the petrification of the trolls because it's his provoking them into an argument that keeps them out in the sun.

Suppose there is an exciting scene in which the hero is saved by an avalanche. Lucky for the hero! But luck for the hero is usually bad luck for the plot.

But if we establish that the hero's party has been carefully climbing the mountain, being as quiet as possible because of the danger of avalanches, and then the hero sets off firecrackers, the resulting avalanche is no longer a *deus ex machina.* It is a clever scheme.

THEME

Theme is the answer to "what is this game really about?" It's also the answer to, "why is making this game worth several years of your life?"

The theme is the underlying, universal human truth your story deals with.

Spec Ops: The Line, for example, is about a soldier driven mad by his desire to be a hero. It is about subverting the hero trope we see in most shooters. It is arguably about the American habit of sending troops to help other countries, and how they can do more damage than good.

80 Days is implicitly about colonialism.

Journey is about endurance and solitude.

Papo & Yo is about alcoholism.

Brothers: A Tale of Two Sons is about how people need each other.

Stray is about human hubris.

Lucas Pope's *Return of the Obra Dinn* is about "who are the real monsters?"

Lucas Pope's *Papers, Please* is about how bureaucracy causes good people to do horrible things.

The Witcher 3: Wild Hunt is about fatherhood: Geralt's unwillingness to acknowledge that his foster daughter, Ciri, is now a grownup and must now fulfill her destiny without his protection.

Compulsion's *We Happy Few,* which I wrote, was about memory and denial – how people remember what it suits them to remember, not what actually happened. *Contrast,* which I also wrote, was about fathers and daughters.

We say a game has a theme when the story and the gameplay work together to provoke the player to think about a subject.

Games don't necessarily need themes. *Into the Breach* is chess with mechas and giant alien beetles. Chris Avellone, the writer, is not trying to speak to universal human experience. The game is just good, addictive fun. (Horribly, horribly, addictive.)

You could argue that *Tetris* is "really" about how we all have to fight not to wall off other people. But unless you're writing an essay for AP English, maybe don't.

A game does not need a theme, but themes are valuable. They help the developers create a unified experience. Is this side quest about memory and denial in some way? No? Then cut it. A game with a theme is more likely to stick with the player emotionally after they've stopped playing.

A game may seem to have several themes. Is *Heaven's Vault* about dwindling resources? Or about how the journey is more important than the destination? A game doesn't have to be dogmatic about what its themes are. Let gamers argue that out on the forums.

But the development team should have one single theme that they are focused on supporting. Trying to serve multiple themes is a recipe for muddy storytelling.

Note that a theme is not the same as a moral. The theme of a game can be memory and denial, but the game only has a moral if it explicitly says, e.g., "denying your memories is bad!"

A game doesn't usually need to have a moral. It's usually better to let the player draw their own conclusions about the theme. I prefer to present the player with a choice. *Is* denying your memories bad? What if you've done something so horrible you can't live with yourself?

There may be one character making an argument in one direction, and another character enunciating the opposite. ("What have the Romans ever done for us?" "Well, aqueducts.") What gives a game a theme is that the events in it touch on a key question. It doesn't have to answer that question.

SUBVERTING TROPES

Tropes are story structures that are familiar to us. The crazy guy and the normie working together. The old veteran and the by-the-book probie. The hero who must sacrifice himself. The hit man's one last job.

Tropes work. Tropes are not bad.[6]

But tropes are familiar. You need to make them fresh. You can do that by subverting them and making them your own.

The crazy guy and … the other crazy guy. The hero who must sacrifice himself, but decides, y'know what, no. The hit man's high school reunion.

A good story is surprising yet inevitable. When all is said and done, the finale should make sense. It was inevitable that we would end up here. But how we got here is unexpected, and maybe the final outcome is not what we expected.

A BRIEF NOTE ABOUT THE HERO'S JOURNEY

The Hero's Journey is a well-known trope in games and screenwriting. An anthropologist named Joseph Campbell wrote a famous book, *The Hero with a Thousand Faces*, where he shows how many hero stories among many cultures share similarities. They start with the hero having an ordinary life. He (almost always he) receives a Call to Adventure. But he Refuses the Call. But then something forces him into the adventure, where he travels to another world, meets a scarecrow, a cowardly lion, and –

--er, anyway, many hero stories have similar beats.

The Hero's Journey is particularly famous because George Lucas used it to plot the first Star Wars movie, *A New Hope*.

Non-writers like The Hero's Journey because it is a simple formula for writing a plot, and they can check your story against it, and say something clever about, "Where would you say The Inmost Cave is in your story?"

Because, of course, to be a good story, it has to hit all the steps, including The Inmost Cave.

The thing is, The Hero's Journey was meant to be descriptive, not prescriptive. Even Joseph Campbell doesn't maintain that any hero stories have *all* the steps. Just that, taken as a group, here are some common steps in the journey of an average mythological hero.

It is not a formula for writing a story. Especially now that so many games and screenplays adhere to it, it is definitely not a formula for writing a fresh story.

It does not particularly make sense for a game. For example, the hero of a game does not need to Refuse the Call to Adventure. The player just paid $80 for the game. They are damn well going on that adventure.

It is not even universal in hero stories. Jack does not Refuse the Call; he goes right up that beanstalk the moment it grows.

Because some of the steps in the trope, like Return with the Elixir, are bafflingly vague, it is often possible to fit The Hero's Journey to any old story – just like the tired notion that every movie should have three acts. Sure, every story has a beginning, middle, and end. Try writing a story without them. I'll wait.

But many great movies do not break neatly into three acts. *The Incredibles*, for example, breaks neatly into seven acts, like an old-style TV movie. Sure, you can label stretches of any movie Act One, Act Two, and Act Three. But it is not a useful exercise for a writer.

Do not use The Hero's Journey to come up with your plot. If you are asked to do that, feel free to tell them that I told you not to. If somehow that doesn't work, write the story your way, and then label the different parts of it with the steps of The Hero's Journey. Some of them might even fit!

There is a meme of a safety poster reading, "It has been 0 days since someone mentioned the Hero's Journey." There is a Discord channel called Reset the Sign. That's how writers feel about The Hero's Journey.

The only prescriptive chart you need to follow is the one in Figure 2.2.

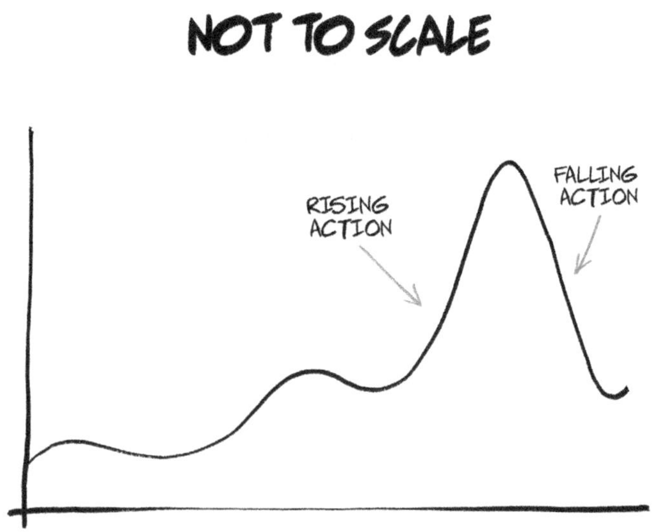

FIGURE 2.2 Not to scale.

Every great story has rising tension, a climax, and a resolution. That's it.

NARRATIVE VS. STORY

Note that "story" is only part of the narrative. Narrative is everything in a game that makes us care about what happens in the game world. It's what makes us feel immersed in the game world. Whether the townsfolk use horse carts or levitating rugs to get around is narrative. Whether they have different accents is narrative. The words on the sides of the inevitable crates are narrative. Depending on the game, world building may be as important or more important than the main story. Sometimes all we have to engage the player is world building.

NOTES

1 Interview with author on author's blog, *Complications Ensue*, October, 2020. https://complicationsensue.blogspot.com/2020/10/jon-ingold-part-three.html.
2 Interview with author in author's blog *Complications Ensue*, December 1, 2020.
3 Though arguably he is right to be thoughtful. See David Ball's excellent *Backwards & Forwards: A Technical Manual for Reading Plays.*
4 https://kfmonkey.blogspot.com/2005/12/writing-action-scenes.html.
5 Jane Espenson's blog Jane in Progress, 10/31/2006: "There's More Than One Way to Bait a Schmuck," https://janeespenson.com/archives/00000230.php.
6 https://tvtropes.org/pmwiki/pmwiki.php/Administrivia/TropesAreTools.

CHAPTER 3

World Building

Video game narrative isn't just the characters. It is also what happened in the world before we got here and why it behaves the way it does.

Video games create entire worlds. They are almost anything you can imagine. Spectacular things, from underwater Ayn Randian planned communities to steam-punk whale oil empires, to islands of cutesy animal people, to modern Alaska. They tend to feel spectacular.

Turns out, making an outlandish world isn't much harder than making a mundane one. A movie can go out and shoot a city street. But every discarded beer can on a video game street has to be lovingly modeled by an environmental artist. It's no easier to make a tiger than a mechanical *Tyrannosaurus rex* for *Horizon Zero Dawn*. So why not make the *T. rex*?

They don't *have* to look spectacular. The graphics of *The Return of Obra Dinn* and *Papers, Please* are basic. But they create convincing and moving worlds.

World building often creates a world story, which is the backstory for the world. How did this world get this way? How is it different from our world? It is answering the question: what is it about this world that makes me want to spend time in it?

RELATABILITY AND STRANGENESS

That's usually a combination of relatability and strangeness. To care, we need a world familiar enough that we feel we know the rules.

Take the gritty universe of *Alien* – the movies and the games. There are starships and xenomorphs – strange. But there is always the

DOI: 10.1201/9781003589068-3

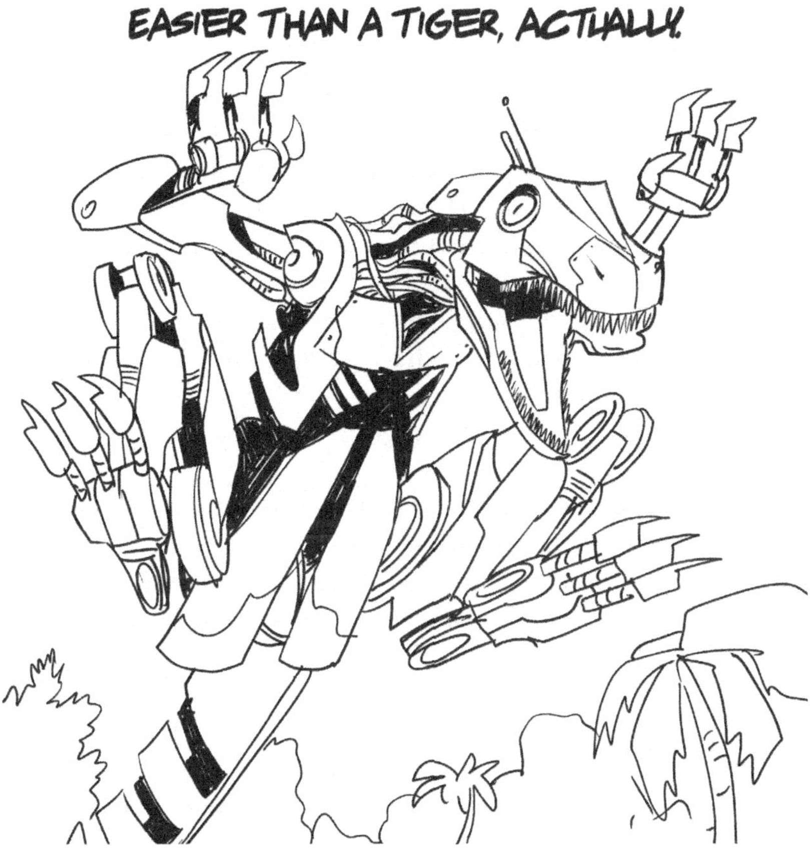

FIGURE 3.1 Easier than a tiger.

Weyland-Yutani company, and crew members are on contract. It is perfectly willing to cancel their paychecks if they don't do what they're told. Ever had a lousy job you needed to keep? Relatable.

Unpacking is about taking things out of boxes and putting them where they belong in your new apartment in different stages of your life. It's a task that is extremely relatable. We know all the objects that come out of the boxes, and we know what they mean. And when we discover that there is simply nowhere for the player character to put her own framed photographs in her boyfriend's apartment, we know what that means, too. The strangeness is that we are unpacking for someone else, someone that we come to know only through unpacking her changing stuff into her changing homes.

Don't Starve is about surviving in an increasingly hostile world. We know what it's like to be hungry and we know what it's like to be cold. We're scared of the dark. That's all relatable. The strangeness comes from having life boiled down to the survival loop and, of course, the sentient pigs.

Both relatability and strangeness come from culture. It's rare to find a game that invents a completely new world with rules we've never seen before, and that sort of game rarely moves players emotionally.

We grow up hearing stories about knights and dragons. We have expectations about what knights and dragons are like, and knights who behave the way knights are supposed to behave are relatable. We can imagine ourselves wearing armor and fighting with sword and shield. We can relate to characters who want honor and glory even if those aren't the values driving our own lives.

We have no trouble relating to Mario trying to save the princess, because everybody knows princesses need saving.

A lot of game worlds are riffs on our culture and our history. They are familiar enough that we feel we know them, and strange enough that we've never been able to visit them in real life. *Crusader Kings* is about medieval dynastic politics and war. If you're a fan of medieval history, it allows you to visit. *Grim Fandango* is set in the world of the Mexican Day of the Dead. Any number of game worlds exist in the King Arthur cycle – *Elsinore*, *Pendragon*, etc. And, of course, there are the zillion games riffing on J. R. R. Tolkien's *Lord of the Rings* books – *Baldur's Gate*, *Dragon Age*, *Dwarf Fortress* – which in turn were riffing on European legends. Dwarves are familiar (and somehow, canonically Scottish). Elves are familiar. Orcs are familiar.

Black Myth: Wukong is a hit in China because it's the first significant AAA game sold in the West riffing on Chinese myths and legends. The opening cinematic is a riff on a legend Chinese players have seen in dozens of story books, TV shows, and movies.

The world of *Black Book* comes out of Slavic folklore. Part of the ongoing attraction of the *Assassin's Creed* games is their careful resurrection of places like Renaissance Florence and Revolutionary Boston.

Strangeness is where the game world differs from what's canonical in our culture or our real life. Strangeness is how we twist canon and make it fresh.

The *Shadowrun* world mashes up two culturally familiar worlds. It has orcs, dwarfs, and elves from Tolkien and European fairy stories. And it has secret agents and special teams and sneaking into secure locations from spy novels and heist movies.

We all know about dinosaurs. In *Horizon Zero Dawn*, the dinosaurs are robots. We all know about zombies. The necroids of *Dead Space* are zombies in space.

The world of *The Last of Us* is, "what if zombies, but from fungus?" The world of *Banner Saga* is, "what if Vikings, but alien robots?" The world of *80 Days* is, "What if Jules Verne, but no colonialism?" The world of *World of Goo* is, "what if structural engineering, but squishy?"

Strangeness for its own sake is not that compelling. Strangeness in support of a theme can be. *Bioshock*'s very strange world of Rapture didn't come randomly. It is an imagined implementation of Ayn Rand's harsh Objectivism philosophy. *Papers, Please* speaks to political systems that require people to do cruel and immoral things – dictatorships, say, and health insurance companies.

If there is a theme (and I hope there is), the world story is going to be critical to it.

When I came on board *We Happy Few* as Narrative Director, we knew we wanted to create a groovy 1960s England (relatable) where everyone was taking drugs and wearing happy face masks (strange). We had to retro-engineer *why* they were all covering their faces and popping pills.

We decided that they had all done a Very Bad Thing during the War, and they couldn't stand remembering it. The theme of memory versus denial grew out of those suppressed memories; the stories of the three player characters came out of that theme.

Defining and then conveying the world story is a big part of our job. Ideally, we get to do it as the game is a-building. Sometimes the artists and level designers go off on a toot for a few years and we're called in to see what sense we can make of what's already been done.

WORLD STORY IS NON-LINEAR

The main character's story is usually linear. Even when the game is an open world, like *Fallout* or *Ghosts of Tsushima*, there is a linear main quest line. There may be side quests, but those, too, are linear.

World stories are almost always non-linear. You pick up clues here and there about what the world is like, and you build up a story in your head.

Sometimes the main quest line is *about* finding out what makes the world the way it is, as in *Subnautica, The Return of the Obra Dinn, Horizon Zero Dawn, Book of Hours,* and *I Was a Teenage Exocolonist.*

ENVIRONMENTAL NARRATIVE

Environmental narrative is, broadly, what the world looks like. What do you see around you? Like an archeological site, an old city, or a ghost town, what is there now suggests what came before.

In *Every Day We Fight*, the city of Acacia is filled with aliens and their mechanisms. That's the main story. But we also see evidence of the Terragonian invasion that preceded that: an abandoned military hospital, houses destroyed by artillery, and so on.

Are there ancient ruins? (*Zelda, Dark Souls, Hollow Knight, Tomb Raider, RiME, Ico.*) Then we know that there was a civilization that thrived and then died before the game epoch.

Are there ruins from our present, now decayed? (*Fallout, Last of Us, Horizon Zero Dawn.*) This world is a possible future of ours.

Are there futuristic ruins? (*Halo, Outer Wilds, Assassins Creed, Biomorph.*) That may mean aliens were there, but are gone now; though in *Stray*, the humans are gone now, and only cats, robots, and hideous rat-sized bacteria are left.

Are the ruins current, and still smoking? Then we know that enemies recently destroyed the place. Are we in a half-destroyed city, as in *This War of Mine*? Then we get that we're in a war zone.

If I seem preoccupied with ruins, well, there are a lot of ruins in games. A ruin can convey a lot of meaning without requiring lots of NPCs running errands, talking to each other, and engaging the player.

Environmental narrative can exist on a smaller scale, as are environmental scenarios: a handful of game assets laid out so that the player can tell something happened.

Let's suppose you find a conch shell in the middle of a desert. If it's stuck in sedimentary rock, maybe this desert was once ocean. If it's half-buried in sand, or in a cave, someone must have carried it there. Was there a trade route here once?

Each of the golden statues in *The Forgotten City* shows us a moment from the city's past – whatever was happening when the person broke the rules and turned into a statue. Each room in *The Remains of Edith Finch* tells you the story of the Finch who lived there once. A bomb crater in *War*

FIGURE 3.2 Every vault tells a story.

Stories: The Caribou Trail shows you what's left of a squadron of young Irish soldiers who never made it back to their own lines. That tells you something of the war our heroes are in.

The *Fallout* games do a great job of conveying the story of a vault by what's left in the vault – skeletons, gear, graffiti, etc.

DECALS

A three-dimensional environmental narrative is expensive. Unless you can make a scenario using assets you already have, everything has to be modeled, and modeling is a lot of work.

It's cheaper to convey the world story through decals, that is, two-dimensional textures that can be slapped on objects in the game. These can include billboards, posters, and graffiti.

The posters in *Dishonored* tell you all about the whale-oil-based economy of Dunwall. The flying city of Columbia in *Bioshock Infinite* is plastered with propaganda posters warning us of the False Prophet, which in turn warns us that we are in a theocratic police state. The graffiti in *Portal* is iconic.

The posters in *We Happy Few* remind you that only a Downer would fail to take their Joy and that "Spankers" are there to electrocute Downers.

You can also slap decals on three-dimensional objects like cans, barrels, and the inevitable crates. Brand names in a game can tell you a lot about the world. In one game, we had a lot of fun making up fictional Southern brand names (though they were nixed in the end by legal!).

You get the idea. Please excuse me while I get myself another Nuka-Cola.

FIGURE 3.3 Early draft.

READABLES, ETC.

Of course, world story can be conveyed via text. *Baldur's Gate* and *Skyrim* both have lots of collectible books about their world's lore. *Dark Souls*, *Elden Ring*, and other Fromsoft games typically have most of their lore hidden in the descriptions of collectible items.

Really, any narrative delivery system can be hijacked to convey world story instead of the main story. Characters can recount the world's history in dialog. My friend Anna Megill wrote a series of disturbing kid's puppet shows for *Control*. *Threshold Kids* explain the "science" behind the game's paranatural topics.

GAME BIBLES

A game's "narrative bible" is a document intended to explain the game world, its characters, and their powers. It is intended to be a compendium of all the narrative decisions made so far. Someone coming on to the project ought to be able to read it and know what the narrative is.

Game bibles are almost never kept up to date, so they become unreliable and are soon disregarded. But there's another problem: sometimes one or more writers run amok with the world story. Ever since Tolkien started *The Lord of the Rings* by inventing entire languages and writing a doorstop-heavy book of lore, folks think that's the gold standard.

A heap of lore is not necessarily useful to a game. Often, little of it supports the game's theme or characters. The writer is just letting their imagination run amok.

Consequently, if an artist or level designer does read the backstory document, and throws something into the game based on it, sometimes they are not reinforcing the main story or theme, but muddying it.

Moreover, when you write a ton of lore first, it becomes hard to remember how much of it you have actually put into the game. You think, "Oh, I already wrote that, didn't I?" But it's not in anything player-facing.

Fortunately, most devs don't read backstory documents. Producers and creative directors are fond of asking for backstory documents, but artists are not fond of reading them. People like to be told a story, and most backstory documents are just recitals of things that happened.

At best, other developers will simply ignore the bible. I spent a few weeks writing a long chronicle for a game, and I doubt anyone read it except for the creative director and the narrative team.

Aaron Sorkin, talking about his TV series *The West Wing*, explained:

> I don't like making decisions until you have to make them.... I don't like talking about ... how many brothers and sisters does Bartlet have, are his parents still alive? ...[I]f you have a really good story for Bartlet and his father then, well, now his father's alive.... But if you want to tell stories about sort of the ghost father, and living with the idea that Bartlet's father never liked him, well, now he's died. It wasn't until I wrote "Two Cathedrals" – the second season finale – that we knew Bartlet's father was physically abusive.[1]

There's no point in deciding too many details about the backstory until you know what you need that backstory to be. The backstory should be driven by the needs of the story, not the other way around.

I am wary of spending time writing game bibles. I'd rather spend time writing descriptions of things that will actually go in the game.

Environmental narrative, for example. What is scratched on the walls of that cave? What is in that basement? What is strange about the ruins on the hilltop? What do the names of things tell you about this world? What folk story does that beer label refer to? Why are those tankards shaped so erotically?

We generally put backstory in a game to create a sense of immersion. But what creates a sense of immersion? The recital of historical facts? Or bits and pieces of the environment that hint at a broader world? The real world is full of symptoms of historical events, while the historical events, the causes, are buried in books.

We are used to running into hints of the past; we like speculating about what they mean. In my neighborhood in Montreal, you can see the shadows of centuries: a two-story stone wall topped with brick, a diagonal of black pitch running down the side of a building where it used to meet another roof, a bricked-up hole that used to be a door, or a window. You can almost see what was there before.

I think that hints of the past are more engaging than pushing detailed history at the player. The player has an imagination; let them exercise it, and they will create a richer, more personal world than you can provide them.

"Show, don't tell" is a screenwriting maxim. "Hint, don't show" might be an environmental narrative maxim. We can only put so many objects into our world, since each has to be lovingly crafted in the computer. But the few that we can afford to build can stand in for thousands of other objects we didn't put into our world. The trick is to leave gaps in the evidence. Don't tell the whole backstory. Leave hints at a backstory – possibly ambiguous hints. (More about ambiguity in my chapter on Dirty Narrative.)

NOTE

1 *On Writing*, Published by the Writers Guild of America East, vol. 18, February 2003.

CHAPTER 4

Player and Non-Player Characters

Player characters are the gloves the player slips on to interact with the game. Non-player characters populate the game world and bring it to life. They interact with the player character, helping or hindering them.

In my first book, *Crafty Screenwriting: Writing Movies That Get Made*, I talk about "retro-engineering" characters from the story. The same technique works for games. The story tells you who your characters need to be.

The protagonist is *defined* by the story. If you have a different story, you need a different protagonist.

The hero should have flaws, and these flaws should be ones that make it difficult to achieve his goal.

In *We Happy Few*, Ollie gives himself a mission to reveal the truth about something that happened during the war. That's more difficult because there is another truth about what happened during the war that he is doing his level best to forget.

In *Shelter*, you are trying to get your kids to safety, but you are a only badger.

If the hero has a **ghost**, then achieving his goal should lay that ghost to rest, even if that isn't what he thought he was trying to do. His need to lay his ghost to rest might be part of the obstacles he faces.

In *God of War*, Kratos is mourning his dead wife. That makes it more difficult for him to bond with his son, Atreus, who has lost his mother.

DOI: 10.1201/9781003589068-4

To open himself up to Atreus's pain would mean experiencing his own pain, and he won't do that. In the end, he takes her ashes to the top of the mountain, and in the process, develops a (slightly) better relationship with his son.

Non-player characters (NPCs), too, are defined by the protagonist and the story. They answer a need that the story has.

Disco Elysium is about a man shattered by his past and unwilling to confront it. Harry Dubois has done awful things. He has got himself blackout drunk so he won't remember those things. Or who he is, for that matter.

Since he can't remember who he is, he needs a **foil**: a second character who can help define him.

Harry is a liar and a drunk. He ignores rules. He's a loose cannon. So, the game gives him an **interlocutor**, a partner, who is none of those things. Detective Kim is honest, sober, and obeys the rules as much as he can. His record is clean. He remembers everything he's experienced. He knows who he is and why it's important to do his job.

He would also be incapable of solving the mystery that Harry Dubois solves with his help. Harry, in spite of his flaws, or maybe because of them, is the only man who can solve it.

In *The Last of Us*, Joel is a man who has lost his teenage daughter. He does not want to ever care about anyone again. So, the game gives him Ellie, a teenage girl who's lost her parents. She's a foil and an interlocutor, too. The whole story is about giving Joel reasons to care about Ellie, until finally, he cares more about her than anyone else in the world.

If the game has an antagonist, the antagonist should be defined by the hero. They are the yin to the hero's yang. *God of War: Ragnarök*'s Kratos is stoic, furious, passionate, sentimental, uncompromising, and determined to achieve his righteous goal only through righteous means. His nemesis is therefore Odin, who is mild-mannered, wily, deceitful, unsentimental, willing to compromise, and determined to win by any means.

The game would not be as compelling if Kratos's nemesis were Thor: another straightforward, sentimental god whose answer to challenges is to smash them with his hammer (Thor, smash!).

NPCS NEED OBJECTIVES, TOO

Video games are almost universally good at giving the player character a strong motivation. They are less good at giving the NPCs motivation.

Why would an NPC need motivation? Why not just have the NPC oppose the player character's objective?

Because that's boring. What creates drama is when both characters want things, and both characters are resisting giving the other what they want. (In fact, that is a good working definition of "drama.")

In the real world, everyone is the hero of their own story. Kids playing a game outside (do kids still do that?) will sometimes give themselves an imaginary narrator ("He shoots! He scores!"), but every conscious human being is concerned with what they want, what they're doing to get it, and the obstacles to their getting it.

NPCs should serve the story. They should resonate with the hero's, er, journey. They may give the player character a mission; they may end up helping the player character accomplish it. But that is only a side effect of whatever it is that they want to do. They should never feel like they are there **in order to** be part of the hero's story. Just like real people, they should all feel like they are the heroes of their own stories. They should have a life of their own.

Distressingly often, they don't. It's too common to come across an NPC hanging around next to the "golden path" the player must take, with nothing better to do than wait around to give the player a mission.

Of course, the player does need to be given missions and needs to find out how to accomplish them. An NPC is a convenient way to do that. But give your NPCs their *own* stories. Sure, they're in the game to ask the player to retrieve the Sacred Teacup from under the nest of basilisks. But give them *another* story, that has nothing to do with basilisks.

Every NPC should have their own story. It doesn't need to be explicit; we don't need to get into the details. But you need to know why we should care about them. What is their goal? What's stopping them from achieving it? What do they stand to gain, or lose? What is the flaw that makes them interesting and human?

What they want can be explicit. ("Bring me ten orc heads, I'm making a chandelier"). But it can also be abstract. An NPC may want love, approval, or respect. They may just want to pick a fight, and lucky day, you came along.

How do they go about getting what they want? Do they use violence? Bargaining? Biting sarcasm? (Nobody said the "how" has to be rational or even likely to succeed.)

FIGURE 4.1 Quest giver.

Are they self-destructive? Do they deal with fear by putting themselves in greater danger? That shows us who they are.

Human beings have different flaws to different degrees. And we all have the virtues of our vices and the vices of our virtues.

Characters are defined by at least one dominant flaw. That flaw shows up by the irrational ways they deal with situations – the less-than-completely-sensible way they attempt to get what they want.

Yes, this applies to fantasy. Just because someone is a dragon is no reason they can't have a recognizable personality or a personal need. Give us a dragon who feels sorry for himself. Give us a dragon who always needs to have the last word. Give us a dragon who yearns to meet a princess who will appreciate his poetry.

Give your NPCs drama. Give them a reason *not* to talk to you, for example. You can communicate just as much quest information by a character saying, “Don’t go up that hill, here’s why” as “Please go up that hill.” Or let it become clear that they have their own secret, naughty reasons for wanting the Sacred Teacup.

As you can imagine, I don’t think NPCs need much in the way of backstory. If they have a reason to talk about their past, then sure. (“I was once an adventurer like you, till I took an arrow to the knee.”) But we don’t need to develop any more backstory than can be shown on the screen, by what they do or say, or what sort of clothes or scars they have. We don’t need to know that their mother took away their rubber ducky when they were four. We just need to know what they want and how they like to go about getting it.

FLAWED CHARACTERS ARE MORE FUN

We like other human beings, in real life, when they do good things for people we care about, particularly ourselves.

We *don’t* care about fictional characters when they do good things. We care about them because of their flaws.

We care about Frankenstein because he’s a tormented monster. We care about Frankenstein’s creature because he’s naïve and vengeful.

We care about Batman because he’s another tormented monster, and the only thing keeping him from being another homicidal maniac is dressing up in the latest high-tech batgear and beating the crap out of bad guys.

In *The Last of Us*, we care about Ellie because she’s a sulky, mouthy teenager. We care about Joel because he’s emotionally crippled by the loss of his daughter and won’t let himself be vulnerable.

In *Disco Elysium* we care about Harry Dubois because he’s a wounded, self-destructive addict.

In *Octodad*, we play an octopus trying to pass as a suburban dad, wearing clothes and living in suburbia. Due to the intentionally ridiculous user interface, he has enormous difficulty doing even the simplest things, such as washing dishes or picking things off the floor. That helplessness makes him adorable.

This doesn’t just apply to fictional characters. It applies to the human beings in your life. Your kids drive you crazy. Your parents reduce you to a 13-year-old. You fall in love with the one who's hard to get. If you have a brilliant co-worker or employee who does everything you ask, you like them, but they probably don't stir your emotions the way your parents and kids do.

What's going on is a bit of psychology called **cognitive dissonance**. When you're stuck with a situation, you try to find reasons it's not so bad. When you're stuck with someone, you look for reasons to forgive their flaws.

I mean, suppose some bounty hunter comes into your lair with a thermal detonator. What can you do? You can't shoot him or the bomb will go off. So you laugh and declare that he is your kind of scum.

That's why it's so hard for us to cut our losses and move on. The more trouble someone is, the more we get wrapped up in their story. The worse their flaws, the more our minds work at liking them. And that's why leaving a bad relationship can seem like waking up from a bad dream. When we finally do bail out, the cognitive dissonance switches off, and we're left with the person's flaws.

THE UNCANNY VALLEY

In animation, there's an effect called the "uncanny valley." We have no trouble feeling sympathy for a cartoon character, even though they look nothing like a person. But an animated character who is too similar to a real human being, but not quite similar enough, becomes creepy. Some people think it's instinctive: one thing that looks human but isn't quite is a corpse, and it's unhealthy to be around corpses.

There's an "uncanny valley" in fictional characters' personalities, too. Real people have flaws. Characters without flaws feel artificial, hence a little bit creepy.

(This was my issue with *Detroit: Become Human*. We're supposed to feel like the androids deserve to be treated like people. But they have no interesting flaws. Consequently, they don't feel human at all.)

I get nervous any time there's a religious figure in a work of fiction who lives up to his religion. Someone who's wise, kind, insightful, self-deprecating, modest…. I'm just waiting for the other shoe to drop. He's probably a child molester, right? Not because religious figures are all child molesters, but because nobody's that perfect. (And because I suspect the writers are up to something.) Either he has a deep dark terrible secret or … he's not really human.

What defines any character is how they do or say irrational things for emotional reasons. How they go about things *illogically.* People doing the rational, logical, sensible thing doesn't make them characters. People doing dumb, or self-destructive, or reckless, things are characters.

A character who leaves the house by the front door could be anyone. Someone who jumps out the window is a character. Someone who responds to being scared of a dangerous man by trying to placate him could be anyone. It's the sensible thing to do. Someone who responds by provoking him is a character. Who does that? (Maybe they want to prove to themself that they're not scared. Maybe they just hate waiting for the other shoe to drop.)

The plot may need characters to do something dumb. Like, stay in the haunted house. To poach an old Richard Pryor routine, a sensible person would be all –

Hero:	Gee, darling, this is a beautiful house, nice neighborhood, good schools, nice weather, we can afford it—
Strange voice:	Getttt ouuuuut!
Hero:	– too bad we can't stay!

But a character's choices can be annoyingly dumb or brilliantly dumb.

Character decisions are annoyingly dumb when it's obvious they happen because the writers need them to. They are driven by the plot. Hank Azaria calls it the "idiot ball" as in, "Who's carrying the idiot ball this week?"

Character decisions are brilliantly dumb when they happen because the characters are human. They make the kinds of dumb mistakes people make. Ideally, they make dumb decisions that reveal what sort of people they are.

For the plot of *Jaws* to work, Peter Benchley needs Quint, Hooper, and Brody to be isolated on the water. If they can call for help, the third act is them drinking in a bar saying, "Whew, that was some big shark, huh?"

So Quint smashes the radio. That's illogical! But his pride is at stake. He's got his back up against the smart-ass scientist and the bossy police chief. He does not want them to call for help; he's taking it as an insult that they want to call for help. If they get a bigger boat, which would obviously be the sensible thing to do, it won't be his boat. It will be someone else's.

So he smashes the radio. It is a brilliantly dumb thing for him to do. It's a great character moment.

We won't care about characters who are perfect. But we will care about characters who are human beings with outsized personalities, who are outrageous in the ways that real people can be outrageous. We can have concocted situations in our games so long as the characters react to those situations in ways that actual human beings would react.

Use a Character Flaw to Make Sense of a Plot Hole

In turn, you can give a character a flaw in order to make sense of a logical problem in your plot.

In early iterations of *We Happy Few*, Arthur couldn't, for level design reasons, immediately take action on learning an important secret.

At first, as I stared at the index cards on the wall, that seemed like a gaping plot hole.

Then I realized he was emotionally weak, and he might react to the secret by getting as drunk as possible. Now instead of a plot hole, it's a character moment; and when another character finally forces him to act, it's another character moment.

Speaking of flaws…

FLAWS

In video games, opponents often come with flaws. Some of the best-drawn characters in video games are the villains. The *Far Cry* games have memorable villains who are different amounts of crazy and evil. Odin in *God of War: Ragnarok* is shameless and charming. GlaDOS in the *Portal* games is insane, homicidal, and adorable.

Allies have flaws less often, and player characters rarely.

But flaws make us care!

Hmmm. I should probably define "flaw."

A flaw is not attitude. Plenty of allies have attitude. They will give you lip. But teammates on your squad will do whatever you ask them to.

"Fight this dragon!"

"Yes sir!"

"In your underpants!"

"Yes sir!"

They are obedient robots. Instruments of your will. Tools. I appreciate my laptop, but I'm not emotionally attached to it.

Allies can have flaws that don't affect gameplay. Indeed, that is the kind most teammates have.

Astarion, for example, in *Baldur's Gate 3*, is a hot mess. He is all red flags. You know you should swipe left, but you know you're going to swipe right. The various gods who help you out in *Hades* have memorable personalities. Bacchus is a drunk. Aphrodite is a sexpot.

But those personalities don't really figure into how they help you (or occasionally fight you).

To be meaningful – to make us really care – a character's flaws should affect gameplay. The character needs to not do what you ask them to. They need to inconvenience the player.

But what about agency?

Traditionally, games have avoided letting NPC allies mess with the player, because that obstructs player agency. Mustn't get in the way of the player doing what they want to do.

Yet enemies and environments get in the player's way all the time. That's the point of a game. Without opposition, there is no game. Pac-Man without ghosts would be a chore. Giving the player an obstacle isn't depriving him of agency; it's just giving him something else to exercise his agency *on*.

Why can't our team members pitch us curveballs, just like in real life? Instead of assets to be leveraged, why can't they be people with their *own* agency?

To leverage cognitive dissonance, a character should be a bit of a pain in the ass. She could even be so much of a pain that you wonder if she's worth keeping on the team – so long as the answer is "yes."

I submit to you that if I can make a character difficult, but not impossible, to live with, then I can make you care about that character. And dealing with that character can be fun, just as dealing with enemies and obstacles and puzzles is fun.

Okay, let's try an example.

You get a new NPC ally. Let's call him "Grout." Grout is terribly good at opening things. He is also forgetful. He forgets your name. He forgets where he put his shoes. He forgets his own birthday.

So far, this is just flavor. Most NPCs have personalities that are just flavor, not gameplay.

Let's say you obtain the Mallet of One-Shot Dragon Stomp. Just the perfect weapon to destroy Alduin, the World Eater.

Unfortunately, when you set out to destroy Alduin, your mallet goes missing. It seems that Grout left it back at the inn. Won't you be pissed off at Grout?

You bet. Your whole strategy for killing Alduin, the World Eater, required that mallet, and now I've gone and screwed that up.

Won't you be pissed off at the game? And even more importantly, at *me*?

Not if, by giving Grout a serious personality flaw, I make the game *more fun* than it would be without it.

Players will put up with challenges if they make the game more fun. They get frustrated only if the challenges turn into chores. As G. K. Chesterton observed, "An adventure is an inconvenience properly considered."

If the players' troubles with their allies are as surprising, challenging, and entertaining as their troubles with their enemies and environment, then players will embrace the story.

HOW CAN WE BUILD FLAWS INTO OUR NPCS?

Make Their Flaws the Story

When you're telling a linear story, you can make their flaws the story.

In *Contrast,* you play Dawn, the invisible friend of an 8-year-old girl named Didi. Her father is Johnny Fenris. He loves her, but he's a screwup and pathological liar. Her mother is a liar, too. The story of the first act is Dawn (the player character) helping Didi discover the truth about some things her mother has lied to her about. If Kat wasn't a liar, there'd be no story.

The second act is about Dawn helping Didi rescue Johnny from mobsters he's borrowed money from. Johnny's being a deadbeat gives Didi the room to become a hero.

In *Papo & Yo*, Papo is your giant doofus of a best friend. He sleeps all the time. You can jump on his belly to bounce up to places you couldn't go on your own. You throw melons to get him to move around. He's harmless.

Except when he eats green frogs. Then he beats the crap out of you.

This is not just a mechanic. It is the core of the game story. Papo's sickness drives you to find a shaman to cure him. You grow attached to Papo because you cannot progress in the game without his help. But he hurts you.

Papo's sickness is an allegory for alcoholism. Vander Caballero's father was an alcoholic, and Caballero made the game to communicate to players what that was like. Until I played *Papo & Yo*, I never had a visceral sense of what living with an alcoholic parent might be like: someone you can't live without, but who hurts you when he's drunk.

Make Character Flaws a Core Game Mechanic

Many games don't have a linear narrative. But you can make flaws into a game mechanic.

In the *Crusader Kings*, your dynasty members' flaws are part of the challenge you strategize around. Your son grows up to be a coward; when you're dead, he'll make a terrible King that everyone will rebel against. Do you arrange an unfortunate accident for him? The Holy Roman Emperor offers his fifth daughter for your son to marry. She is brilliant but homosexual. In game terms, this is a flaw: she is less likely to give you an heir. Do you risk your son marrying her? Characters' flaws make them feel like real people. If they only had virtues, they would not seem human.

In *Ico*, Princess Yorda is incapable of defending herself and can't jump as far as Ico. If she could climb and jump better, she would be irrelevant to the game; because she's weak and helpless, you come to care about her … even if you get frustrated at the sexist stereotype that drives the game.

Reveal an NPC Flaw as a Way of Sending You on a New Adventure

Writers aren't always invited to participate in conceptualizing a game. (I am understating here. I have often been invited, but I've led a life full of blessings.) You can't necessarily base the story on character flaws or build the gameplay around them. You might get hired onto the game that's been in production for years and asked to paint a narrative on it.

Even if you can't control the overall story, you may be able to add a character twist to the story of an individual quest.

Up the Challenge through NPC Character

Traditionally, we up the challenge by throwing more, badass-er goons at the player. We could also up the challenge by giving your teammates flaws. Suppose I have an idea for a really cool mission that would, unfortunately, be too easy because of one particular team member's abilities. But, by using his flaw, I can organically take that one guy out of the picture, allowing me to put that cool mission into the game after all.

Suppose in a squad-based tactical shooter, your teammates keep ribbing your rocket-launcher guy, Jonesy, about his fear of heights. It's just the usual flavor.

Until the mission where you need to send Jonesy up the cell phone tower, and he panics and freezes. Now you're going to have to figure out how to get rid of that tank without a rocket launcher.

Emergent Flaws

Now we're getting out of "best practices" into experimental territory.

NPCs could have flaws that crop up in non-scripted situations.

For example, an NPC could be programmed to be reckless – she will charge into battle the moment she spots an enemy.

Or alcoholic – she will charge into any bar.

Maybe your one teammate is a kleptomaniac and can't be left alone near a store or she'll get caught stealing, and you'll have to break her out of jail.

You could have a Krogan teammate who likes to pick fights with bureaucrats. A character who is brave against monsters but terrified of fire. A character who is so gallant he will never strike the first blow against a woman, no matter how evil she is.

A dwarf and an elf who will kill each other if you leave them alone together. Or maybe they like each other better than they like you.

A character who is terribly slow and shaky before he's had his coffee in the morning.

All of these flaws could be programmed into an NPC's behavior. All of them humanize your teammates and give you a richer experience with them. If you have a Krogan teammate, you better leave him back in the spaceship when you're visiting functionaries at the Citadel. If you have a gallant teammate, you can't count on him sniping a female guard from afar. If you have a kleptomaniac teammate, better not go near that fancy dagger store, unless you think she can get away with it.

You wanted to head up a team, well, we're going to give you the experience of managing a team. It's harder than you think.

Caveats:

- NPC character flaws can never make it impossible for the player to progress.
- Character virtues need to compensate for character flaws. Cognitive dissonance only works if you're not willing to part with the NPC.

- Ideally, character's flaws *are* character virtues. You can send your klepto pal to steal stuff for you. Your Krogan who taunts pencil-pushers also taunts bosses, drawing their fire.
- If a flawed character puts the player in a real jam, then the payoff needs to be worth it.
- Introduce any flaws early. Ideally when the player is deciding which teammates to choose, but definitely with enough warning that the player can make plans accordingly.

Note that you *could* also give flaws like these to the player character. It's more fraught, because you'd be taking away control from the player whenever his reckless character goes Leeeroy Jenkins-ing into combat.

On the other hand, that's what it means to be reckless: you find yourself in situations you wouldn't have been in if you'd thought things through. Games *could* transport you into a character that behaves differently than you do.

Emotional Gates

You can constrain the player character's movement using emotional gates, rather than only physical ones.

In an early draft of *We Happy Few*, there was a point at which General Byng just could not bring himself to knock on Sally's door. If the player clicks to open the door, Byng reaches for the door, then stops. He tells himself, "Come on, man up and knock!" No matter how many times you click to knock, he won't do it. "Why won't you bloody knock?" he says to himself. The player has to figure out what will give Byng *emotional* permission to open the door.

Some level designers consider this heresy. For some reason, it is perfectly acceptable for a door to be locked until you find the key to open it. But it is not acceptable for the door to be locked until you find the courage to open it.

We accept that super-warrior Commander Shepherd in *Mass Effect* cannot climb over any wall taller than about three feet. Gamers accept that Kratos can smash trolls, but cannot break a window. So why not emotional doors?

After all, emotional doors are more interesting than physical ones. They tell you something about the character. Like a flaw, an emotional wall or door gives us deeper empathy for what they're going through.

You may run into resistance attempting to implement one. I have pitched emotional gates to colleagues. Some level designers categorically reject emotional gates. At other companies, the level designers consider emotional gating just another tool to define level flow.

Allow the Player to Define His Character through Actions

In an RPG, the player can decide whether their character is a dwarf or a githyanki, a monk or a warlock, and who their supernatural patron is. They can define their character's background to some extent. However, we can also allow the player to make these choices through actions.

In *Mass Effect*, the player, by choosing goody-goody dialog options or damn-the-rules ones, can rack up a score as a Paragon or Renegade, which in turn gives the player access to additional dialog choices. Their Captain Shepherd is a different person than your out-of-the-box Captain Shepherd.

But it could also have led to giving Captain Shepherd different backstories. They could have been first in their class in the Academy, or they could have been a smuggler in an earlier career. (Yes, you get to choose three backstories for Captain Shepherd as is; this would be a less direct but more immersive mechanism for choice.)

The mind interprets stories holistically. We piece together a chronological order even if we don't get the pieces in chronological order. Even if we see the effects first, once we discover the causes, we make a story out of it. That's why it's a classic technique in storytelling to start somewhere in the middle, and only reveal the beginning halfway into the story – whether it's *The Odyssey* or *Casablanca.*

Suppose the player character is always charging into battle. NPCs might begin to talk to him as if they consider him brave – if they like him – or reckless – if they don't. If he is cautious, they might call him wise – if they like him – or cowardly – if they don't.

They might even start to recount things that they did with the character – reckless adventures they did with him if the player makes him reckless, or wise things the character did for them if the player makes him wise.

Because storytelling is four dimensional, we can ground the player's personality in his past. If the player chooses to play his character recklessly, we can tell him about how his character had a brother everyone looked up to – a Boromir to his Faramir – and that's why his character is so anxious to prove that he's brave. Or, that his brother shamed the family, and *that's* why he's so anxious to prove he's brave.

Speaking of backstories…

CHARACTER BACKSTORIES

How do we find out who the characters are? Two ways: what they do and say; and backstory. A character's backstory might come through in wanted posters, in flashbacks, in things other characters say about them, in the tattered uniform they wear – any narrative delivery system, really.

What characters do and say in the game is generally more powerful in creating character than anything in backstory. It's certainly more immediate.

Fortunately, there is no need to present a character's backstory until the player knows who they are and is wondering how they got that way. Human beings are perfectly capable of absorbing stories non-linearly. Very often we meet a person and only later find out about their past. Our experience of them grows and changes over time.

That's the best way to present character backstories, too. We need to see the character behave in the present before we care about how they got to be the way they are. We should only learn about their past once we have a sense of them in the present.

Backstories often show up in the game bible. There may be a page in Confluence on a character and their past. But I am wary of backstory in game bibles. Your fellow developers may assume that because the character's story is in the game bible, it is in the game, too. I have seen people put a lot of effort into game bible backstories, almost none of which got into the game.

Incidentally, because we can absorb backstories non-linearly, that means they can be malleable. Some games let you choose from a variety of backstories. In *Mass Effect,* you can give your Commander Shepard different backgrounds:

Spacer:	Both of your parents were in the Alliance military….
Earthborn:	You were an orphan raised on the streets of the great megatropolises covering Earth….
Colonist:	You were born and raised on Mindoir, a small border colony in the Attican Traverse.

In Telltale's first *Walking Dead* game, you can choose via dialog options whether the protagonist, Lee Everett, did the murder he was sent to prison for.

A player could also choose their character's backstory via their gameplay. Rather than asking the player to pick Lee Everett's backstory through a dialog option, we could present the player with a choice of killing someone. If he does, the game could decide that he did do the murder. If not, then he's innocent. We could give Commander Shepard three different ways to solve a problem and then decide from the player's behavior whether he was an orphan on Earth, a colonist, or a spacer.

This sort of backstory could allow the player to feel closer to their character. The player who murders someone in-game is probably more willing to play a murderer; the player who avoids killing someone might be happier to play an innocent.

GIVE THE PROTAGONIST ALL THE BEST DRAMA

The player character should motivate the action. Anything that happens should be something they decided to do, or the environment's or their opponents' reaction to something they decided to do.

If someone has a moral choice or a hard decision to make, it usually should be the main character. The character making the moral choice is almost by definition the main character of a story, so they better be the player character!

Be careful if you find one of your NPCs facing a difficult moral choice. If you can, find a way to turn that into a choice that the player character must make.

Likewise, if someone is going to have an emotional moment, it's generally better for it to be the player character. That doesn't mean they have to *show* their emotion. They don't have to talk about their feelings. A lot of video game heroes are laconic and stoic. They don't show their emotions much, and they don't like to say much. They are doers, not sayers.

We just need to know they're having the emotion. That can be a profound sigh or a wry smile. That can also be another character letting the player know the emotion that the player character is having, and why. "You miss him, don't you." Or just hanging a lantern on the fact that they're having an emotion: "You okay?"

If someone's going to make an argument, it should be a main character. If you have a squad or party, then it's better for one of them to argue a point than for someone to make that point who we're never going to see again. The secondary characters should only say things that only they could say.

In TV, the core cast are the characters we see every week. Sometimes you need a guest star to trigger dramatic situations for the core cast: the criminals and victims in a cop show, the patients in a doctor show. But the show *is* the core cast.

Likewise, the story in a game is the player character and (if they have one) their party. The story serves them. The spotlight must be on them.

NPCS IN DIFFERENT WORLDS

It's important to remember that your NPCs are *people*. Even when they are not actually human beings, they should come across as people.

If you are writing a space station, bear in mind that most of the people on it are not involved in your main plot. Even if robots are planning to destroy all sentient life in the galaxy, a lot of people are going to pretend that's not happening, because they can't handle it, or it gets in the way of their other goals.

Some people adore heroes, but most people don't, or only do when they're in a crowd. (After all, a hero is someone who gets all his friends killed.) Have people be rude to the protagonist, not because they hate the protagonist or want to stop them, but just because they're having a bad day.

There is a tendency to have characters defined by their situations.

Say, for example, you're an outcast. Members of The Tribe are mean to you. The character you play is, naturally, spunky, and doesn't let the meanies get her down.

But suppose you were a Muslim or a trans person in South Carolina now. You are made to feel that you do not fit in; some people are mean to you. You are wary of mobs of people.

But one-on-one, people are mean to different degrees and in different ways. Some will mock you. Some will assault you for no good reason. Some will pretend you don't exist, because they're not fundamentally mean and they don't want to have to be mean to you. Some will be mean if other people are around, but nice to you if other people are not. Some will apologize for all the others.

We expect characters from the 20th and 21st centuries to be people with personalities. Their attitudes are *colored* by their situation; they're taught to react to you a certain way. But people are different. Some people are angry and just looking for someone to take it out on. For some, duty is important, and they might hurt you but only because they think they're supposed to; it's not personal.

I miss that in a lot of fantasy, historical, and sf games.

I can't wait for the cave man game where you meet a Neanderthal, and he's a bit of a joker, but, you realize, actually kind of an asshole.

Real people always have their own stories going on. I can't wait till I'm playing a prehistoric game, and I meet a member of the Other Tribe, and she's really upset because she just broke up with her boyfriend and she has 99 problems and she couldn't care less about me.

In A. A. Milne's *Winnie the Pooh*, the animals are people. When you meet Eeyore, he's a self-pitying mope. In fact, he is such a specific self-pitying mope that I feel positive that, if I'd gone to a garden party at A. A. Milne's house, I'd have been able to figure out which of his friends A. A. was making fun of.

So if there are three kids from the tribe harassing the playing in a prehistoric or post-Apocalyptic game, then maybe one of them is really intent on hurting you, and obviously angry at your very existence. But a second kid is trying to pull him away because she was enjoying the game they were playing and you're nothing to her. And another is obviously upset at what the first one is doing, but doesn't want to rock the boat.

Just because you're writing historical or prehistoric characters doesn't mean you can't write people. Modern homo sapiens – meaning humans you could dress up and put in the subway and they'd look completely normal – have been around for at least a hundred thousand years. A hundred thousand years ago, they probably believed the mountain was a god, the stream was another god, and so on. But some of them were really nice people, and some of them were jerks, and some of them you had to catch on a good day, and some of them were egotistical. Some of them wanted to be chief of the tribe, some just wanted to get with the ladies or the men, some were no use for anything day to day but okay in a pinch, and some were smart and sarcastic and useless in a scrap.

And I guarantee you that kids in those days didn't listen to their elders as much as their elders listened to *their* parents, because people have been complaining about *that* since apes learned to talk.

Seriously, we have Roman letters saying, "What's up with kids these days?" And the oldest known customer complaint is on a clay tablet that dates to 1750 BC. God damn it, Ea-nāṣir!

When you're writing aliens, other species, or people from other times and places, try writing them like *specific people that you know.* Write them so specifically that your friends will recognize them. Give them the flaws of the people you're basing them on.

And then, and only then, put on the wench dress, or the toga, or the pointy ears.

RESEARCH

Do you need to research your world? I think so. Even if it is a fantasy world, it is probably based on some human society. Most fantasy worlds are based on medieval Europe. Even alternate history worlds are based on a real world. Steampunk is based on Victorian England. *We Happy Few*'s Britain was based on groovy Swinging London, circa 1964.

Of course, the player probably doesn't know whether Victorian England did or did not have, say, elevators or peanut butter. (After 1870 and 1895, it did.)

Did the Romans have stirrups? No. Did medieval folks have homing pigeons? Yes. Did Swinging London have blue LEDs? No, before 1972 the only LEDs were red.

But here's the odd thing. *The audience doesn't know, but it knows.*

That is, they know when it's *wrong.* They don't know why, but something bothers them. They don't quite believe the world. Maybe they're not thinking, "This world doesn't quite make sense, does it?" But they won't engage with it emotionally on the same level as a world that feels truthful to them.

So, research is important.

You don't have to be fanatical about being period accurate. You can probably get away with throwing firebombs from your trebuchets. What's important is that the *shape* of reality feels real. Add in details that tell the player, "It's okay, the developers did their research." If they feel they can trust you, they will engage more emotionally with your world.

Where a lot of period world building falls apart is when writers assume that the people of the past were different from us now. Just because medieval rich folk liked to hang religious paintings on their walls doesn't mean everyone was devout. It just means it was good to be seen to be devout. They were definitely just as interested in getting laid. There is an awful lot of "swiving" going on in the *Canterbury Tales.*

Put readables in that are moms nagging their sons to come home, badly written love poems, shopping lists, and break-up letters. Have an environmental scenario that hints that one of the guardsmen is a lousy shot. Have an ambient conversation about how someone is worried about their daughter, who just wants to have fun and refuses to settle down.

CHAPTER 5

Linear vs. Dynamic Narrative

When non-gamers think about game stories, they often assume that games have branching stories. The player makes choices, and different things happen, and the world changes.

Some brilliant games do have full-on branching, where the story goes in one direction if you choose x but in a completely other direction if you choose y. But it is not all that common. Why?

Branching stories get crazy fast. If you give players even 5 binary choices, that gives you 32 endings. Eight choices mean 1,024 endings.

That sound you hear is your producer running screaming out of the room.

It is very hard to think of even 32 satisfying ways to end a story, let alone 1,024. I know. I wrote a game called *Stories: The Path of Destinies* with 5 choices and 32 endings.

In the best stories, the seeds of the ending are in the beginning. If the hero achieves something at the end, then the beginning sets up their need to achieve that thing. If they lay their ghost to rest, then they begin by being troubled by that ghost. If they right a wrong, the story begins with the wrong being inflicted. If they *fail* to right a wrong, the story still has to begin with the wrong being inflicted, so that it's heartbreaking that you weren't able to right it.

(*Failing* to right a wrong is infinitely more common in novels and movies. If you can't win it, is it even a game?)

DOI: 10.1201/9781003589068-5

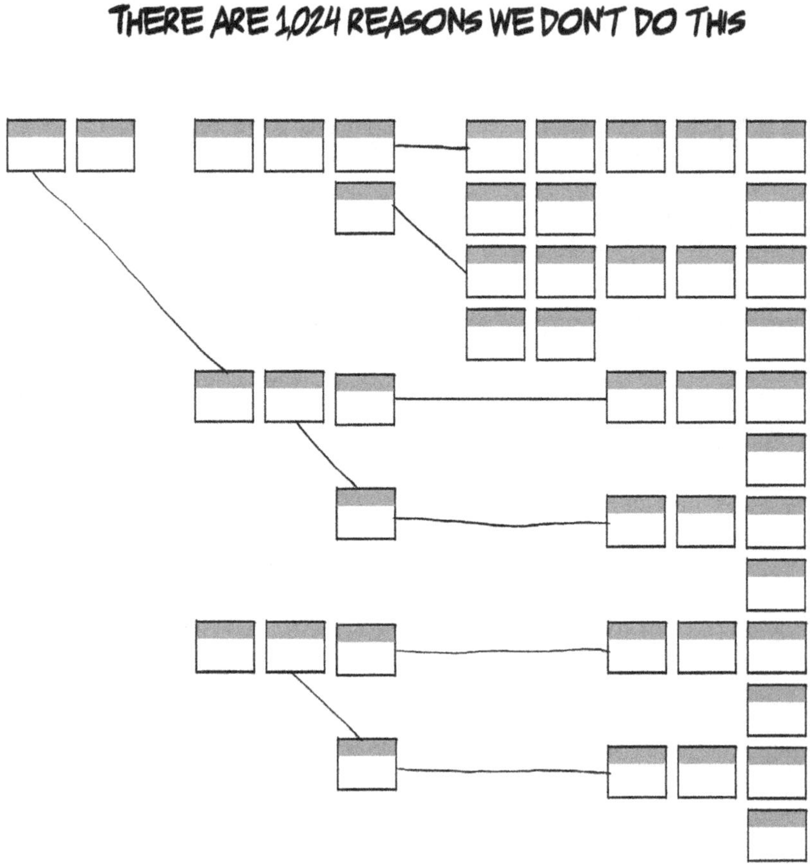

FIGURE 5.1 Charts 3.

Whatever we set up in the beginning, there's going to be one ending that perfectly resolves it. So, any *other* ending will be less than completely satisfying. Branching stories can give you lots of pretty good endings, but only one great ending.

Also, more practically, 32 endings mean there's a lot of content the player will never see. That's inefficient. Writers may not mind writing all those endings – hey, we're getting paid to write! – but producers hate paying to make content the player won't see. The player doesn't want to pay for 80 hours of gameplay and then end up only playing 8 hours.

We can resolve the content problem to some extent by requiring the player to play through the story tree multiple times in multiple different ways. That's what we did on *Stories*.

On the first playthrough, the only endings available have our hero Reynardo failing disastrously in various outlandish ways. He can't reach *any* win condition at first. Only after multiple playthroughs, making different choices each time, can he save the world and win the princess.

So, our game had only one satisfying ending where you "beat" the game. We could have given the game some "pretty good" alternate endings, but that would mean the player might finish the game without getting the *best* ending.

Every game teaches you something about making it. I learned why we rarely employ branching narrative.

Because branching narrative presents such challenges, many (most?) story-driven games have a fundamentally linear narrative. There's only one way to finish *The Last of Us, Braid, Journey,* or tens of thousands of other games.

Many AAA games have oodles of side quests where you can score experience and gear, but the main story is linear. You can sail the high seas capturing ships to your heart's content in *Assassin's Creed: Black Flag,* but as far as the story goes, there's just one way to get to the end.

But fully branching and fully linear are not the only choices. Games use a variety of strategies to give the player meaningful choices without driving their producers mad or broke. They include:

- Only a few branch points.
- Pruned branching trees, aka the gauntlet.
- Hub-and-spoke.
- Faction.
- Branch-and-bottleneck.

FEW BRANCH POINTS

The simplest way to keep a branching tree manageable is simply not to branch more than a few times.

There are two meaningful choices in *We Happy Few.* At the very beginning of the game, Arthur Hastings is afflicted with troubling memories. He ponders taking his Joy pill, which will wipe them away. If he does take it, he forgets those memories, and the game ends immediately.

If he doesn't take it, then at the very end of the game, the mysterious Chief Inspector Peters, who "patrols the boundaries," offers the same choice. By now Arthur has a lot to forget. If he does take the pill, we cut to him happily riding a playground pony; if not, he completes his destiny.

There is one choice in *We Happy Few: Roger and James in They Came from Below*, at the very end: whether to kiss James or not. If Roger kisses James, they go off on a new adventure together. If not, Roger leaves James behind.

For *Contrast*, we prototyped another choice at the end. The game was going to allow two different endings. In one, Didi, the little girl you're helping, ends up with her adoptive father, who is loving but a deadbeat. In the other, she goes off with her biological father, who is cold, but will give her a life of adventure.

Rather than having the player explicitly choose which dad Didi ended up with, we would give the player a chance to lead Didi on a safe, but longer path up to the top of a building, or a much shorter path that involved a dangerous jump. Players who chose the dangerous jump would end up with a cold dad and a life of adventure. Players who chose the longer path would end up with the nurturing but feckless dad. Both endings would have been bittersweet.

Compulsion being an indie studio of fewer than ten people at the time, we weren't able to implement that choice system, but I still mourn its loss!

As you can guess, I am fond of choices at the end. They're not expensive. A choice in the middle of the game means a lot of things need to be different, whether those things are stories or quests or environments or other assets. A choice at the end means few things have to change. But they allow the player to own the ending. The player gets to decide what their actions *mean*. You can get a lot of mileage out of a choice at the end.

Depending on what the player has done in *Deus Ex: Human Revolution*, the game allows Adam Jensen, the heavily "augmented" (cyborg) player character to choose one of up to four outcomes for humanity:

- Abandon research into human augmentation.
- Allow research on augmentation technology without regulations.
- Allow research, but under strict regulations.
- Make no choice, and allow humanity to decide.

In *Mass Effect 3*, depending on how many War Assets the player has accumulated, Commander Shepard has up to three "good" choices:

- Destroy: Sacrifice his life to wipe out all synthetic life, including the deadly Reapers, but also the sentient Geth.
- Control: Sacrifice his humanity to control the Reapers and force them to rebuild galactic civilization.
- Synthesis: Sacrifice his identity to merge synthetic and organic life, neutralizing the Reapers.

Red Dead Redemption could easily have ended in a choice. In the game, John Marston sends his son away, dooming himself to be killed by a posse. In the last mission, his son seeks vengeance for his father's death.

The player could have been given an alternative: allow his son to fight alongside him. In that case, perhaps his son would be killed, and he would seek vengeance. Either way, it would be an ending that the player owned.

Of course, a game can have choices other places than at the beginning or the end.

The Witcher 2: Assassins of Kings has one really big choice in the middle. The player may choose whether to aid either Iorveth or Roche. That sends you off into two entirely different second acts, which take place in different maps. However, the overall structure of Act Three is similar regardless of which choice you made.

The game does have 16 possible ending states, based on actions you take, such as whether you rescue the sorceress Triss. But most of the missions are the same, and the endings are mostly just text reported at the very end.

THE GAUNTLET

We can also prune the branching story tree.

Or to use another metaphor: the story is a gauntlet. There are many choices. But for each choice, there is one path to an immediate end to the game – usually meaning failure and death, though it could be an early win. There is one long golden path to victory. There is always one choice that will allow you to continue your journey. Every other choice leads to an early ending, which usually means failure and death.

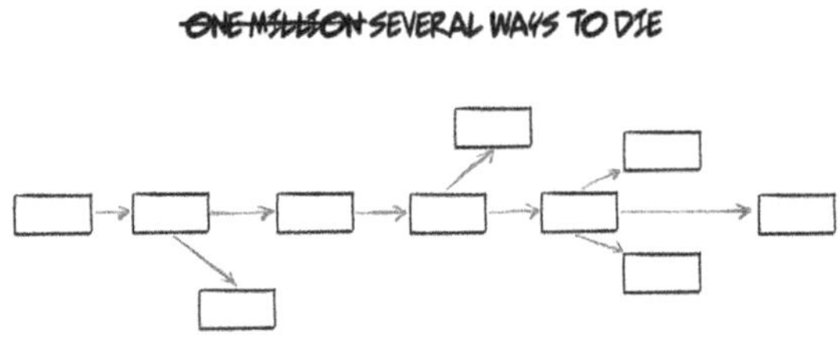

FIGURE 5.2 The Gauntlet.

But the player does get to make choices and feel like they're in command of their player character.

This structure is typical of roguelike games such as *Slay the Spire*, but any game where the player character's death sends you back to the beginning has this structure. In Supergiant Games' *Hades*, Zagreus repeatedly attempts to escape the realm of his father, Hades, the King of the Land of the Dead. Each time he's killed, he goes back to his father's court. But with each playthrough of the gauntlet, you learn more of his story, as you learn not to get killed so fast.

Even when the overall structure of the game is on rails, a few gauntlet-style choices can add meaningful agency for the player.

The first choice in *We Happy Few* is a gauntlet choice.

There is another gauntlet choice at the beginning of *Far Cry 4*. The game begins when you arrive in the country of Kyrat, where you are a nephew of the tyrant, Pagan Min. Your goal is to go to "Lakshmana" in order to spread your mother's ashes. You meet him. He asks you to wait 15 minutes.

Instead, you go wandering through the palace and get caught up in the resistance to Pagan Min, which leads you to supporting one of two pretty awful rebel groups. But if you simply stay in the room for 15 minutes of real-life time, Pagan Min returns and takes you to Lakshmana, which is just behind the palace. You scatter your mother's ashes, and voilà! You won!

In *Baldur's Gate*, there is a point just before the end of the second act where all the characters you need to kill are in one place, and, if you've played your cards right, you have a powerful bomb. If you move fast, you can successfully end the story there. Otherwise, you've got to go through the entire third act to complete the game story.

Are these early endings valuable? Or are they just gimmicks? *We Happy Few*'s early ending makes the point that taking the pill or not is a real choice. *Baldur's Gate's* possible early ending is part of its philosophy of allowing the player to find exploits by working the gameplay environment, just like you could in the real world. They may not carry the emotional impact of taking the game to the natural end of its story. But the player probably tries them only after completing a more traditional run-through. *Far Cry 4*'s early ending is an acknowledgment that both rebel groups you can fight for are arguably no better than the brutal dictator and also that only an idiot would leave the room after a brutal dictator asked them to stay there for 15 minutes.

BRANCH-AND-BOTTLENECK AKA BRANCH-AND-MERGE

Another common branching structure is the "branch-and-bottleneck" story graph.

The story tree branches out, giving the player legitimate choices with consequences. But all the branches lead to the same place, and the consequences don't last past the next bottleneck. The player experiences different stories, but the game developers only have to deliver, say, 2 or 3 times as much content, rather than 32 times as much.

Branch-and-bottleneck is very common in open-world games. The player has a wide choice of quests to fill, but once the story progresses, these quests disappear, leaving only the knowledge, experience, gear, allies, and money the player gained in them.

That sounds like a lot, but it's easy enough to keep track of these things and take them into account in the game mechanics. Asking the game to

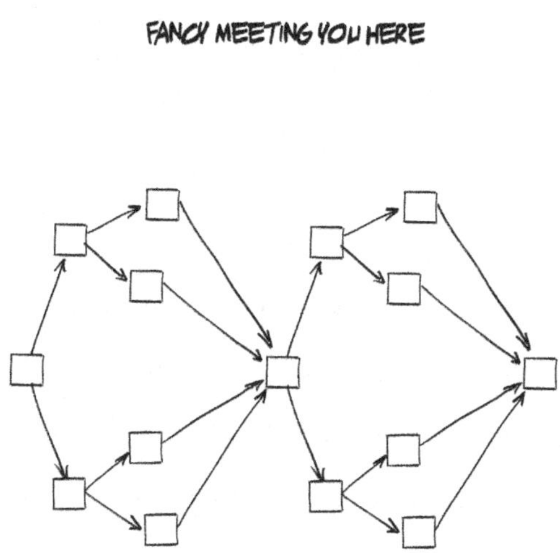

FIGURE 5.3 Branch and bottleneck.

remember what happened and how it happened is the thing you want to avoid.

A simple example is Obsidian's *Pentiment.* The player can choose to talk to different characters as they attempt to solve the murders. But at the end of each act, the game state is simplified, and only the player remembers the choices they made.

Likewise, in Bioware's *Mass Effect 2*, the player can recruit different allies by completing missions. The player can then unlock powers for those allies by completing "loyalty missions." The player is free to run around the galaxy playing all, some, or none of the side missions before the next key story node. But each time the main story moves forward, it does the same thing no matter what missions the player played. For the purposes of gameplay, the game only has to remember which characters you recruited and whether or not they have their special powers. That's a classic branch-and-bottleneck.

STATE TRACKING, AKA FACTIONS

State tracking is an efficient way games can give players a lot of meaningful choices. It is a traditional way of doing narrative in an open world if the design is that the player can back out of any mission at any time, go do something else, and then come back to the mission.

The player can go to a location, trigger a story, single-mindedly complete a mission, and then go on to another location. Or, you can go to a location, trigger a story, back out, go somewhere else where you're already involved in another story, and move that along a little. Then you can come back to the first story. In the meantime, the game has kept track of:

- Who you talked to.
- Whether key lines were said between you and that character.
- Who is hostile to you and will fight you on sight.
- Whether they are still in a state of alarm.
- Who you killed and so removed from the game world.
- How all that affects your standing with various characters and factions in the game.
- Your current objectives.

If that sounds like a lot, it is. State tracking is super hard to do. Writers have to create stacks of conditionals, like:

- If you never met the non-player character (NPC) before, say "Hi there!"
- If you met the NPC before, and are on good terms, say "Hey, you're back!"
- If you met the NPC before, and on bad terms, say "Ohhhhh, wonderful. He's back."
- If you met the NPC before and got into combat with them, say "He's back! Kill him!" and attack.

And that's just for the first line.

By keeping track of key game state information, the game can open and close off quests in ways that make sense for the story. The game can set prerequisites for advancing in the story, or just make certain sidequests available under certain conditions.

In Obsidian's *Fallout* games, you develop a reputation with different factions in the game. In *Fallout: New Vegas*, for example, you might have one relationship with Caesar's Legion, and another one with New California Republic. Having a good reputation with Caesar's Legion will open up new dialog options with members of the Legion, which will open up new quests. Getting to a certain point with the Legion will also destroy any good reputation you had with the NCR and close off dialog and quest options with them. If your reputation gets high enough with Caesar's Legion, the NCR will shoot you on sight.

The multiple ending states of *Witcher 2* depend on state tracking. Did you rescue Triss? Or Anais? Or assist Philippa Eilhart? These choices don't change the gameplay significantly, but they will be reflected in the politics of the game world, as reported in the epilogue.

There can also be ability gates, where certain quests are closed off until you have certain abilities or have reached a certain level. These can be hard gates – the game just won't let you through – or soft – where a character or the game itself asks you if it's really wise to go into that valley when you're only a level 4.

At its best, state tracking can feel immersive. In real life, you have all sorts of relationships with all sorts of people. You may have to build up a friendship with someone before they tell you about an opportunity. Ideally, state tracking can allow us to create a feeling that the player can do anything they want, and the game will respond. Most players won't explore the quirky little low-percentage dialog options. But they like to know they're there; it gives them a sense of ownership of the mainstream lines they actually use. Hopefully, some players will discover some of the strange, quirky little conditionals we built in, and say nice things on social media. Social media about *Baldur's Gate 3*, a huge game with state tracking, is full of "I made these off-the-wall choices and you'll never believe what happened!"

State tracking isn't easy to implement. Every dialog and story option needs to be designed in advance. Inevitably you are creating a huge bunch of content that most players won't see. That's expensive.

Moreover, QA testing for a state tracking game will be complicated. Testers will need to test all sorts of different combinations of states to make sure that your dialog will still make sense. That's why a lot of games seal you into a mission, so that the game only has to keep track of the state of the game when you entered it, and the state of the game when you completed it.

LET THE PLAYER MAKE THEIR OWN STORY

Some successful games give you world elements infused with story-ness and let you play with them. The story is whatever you make happen.

The *Civilization* series, for example, allows you to interact with the leaders of other civilizations. How they treat you becomes a story. ("I can't believe Gandhi nuked me! Again!")

In *Dwarf Fortress*, you can set your little guys' objectives and watch as terrible consequences unfold. For example, if they delve greedily and too deep. You have created a story, in the sense that you picked one or more characters and gave them objectives; the game gives them obstacles and antagonists.

In *Shadow of Mordor*, orc leaders remember when they kill you, and when you kill them, and either mock you or aggro on you accordingly. That's really only bits of a story, but the "nemesis system" makes you care about your orc enemies.

As a game writer, you'd probably rather not work on these games as your involvement will be minimal. But imbuing world elements with story-ness is honest work.

CHANGE THE MEANING BY CHANGING THE BACKSTORY

We can "branch" a story by changing an element of the backstory. Changing a character's past, for example, may only involve changing a line or two of dialog, or a page in a book the player character finds. But it can change the story and its meaning.

For example, in Richard Rouse III's *Church in the Darkness* (2019), the player tries to rescue a loved one from a cult. But is it an evil suicide cult or just a harmless religious sect? The answer is randomized for each playthrough.

The gameplay is the same – you're infiltrating the cult's encampment. That may affect how the players feel about shooting the cultists. It's all very well and good to shoot evil death cultists to rescue your beloved. Murdering flower children, not so much.

We can allow the player to choose between different backstories. As noted before, the first choice in Telltale's *Walking Dead* game is simply whether your character, Lee Everett, did the crime he was sent to prison for. That may affect how the player feels about him and the choices the player makes for him in the playthrough.

EXPLORABLE STORY SPACE

You can create the bits and pieces of a story and allow players to discover them in any order. The *Fallout* games, for example, typically have a minimal main story and a lot of "side content" that the game is really about.

Discovery doesn't have to mean physical traversal of the map. In Sam Barlow's *Immortality*, the player discovers "lost" footage of various events. They probably won't find all of it, but they'll find out enough to figure out what happened.

EMERGENT STORY

"Emergent" gameplay is when you create systems that affect gameplay and allow the player to combine them to get different effects.

The *Zelda* games are the pinnacle of emergent gameplay, where you can, for example, set fire to things, and then use the resulting updraft to launch yourself on your hang glider high up in the air. The gameplay is "emergent" in the sense that the game designers did not create exotic gameplay where hang gliders soar upward over bonfires, as the devs of *Assassins Creed: Brotherhood* did. They created a mechanism where some things can catch on fire, another mechanism where all heat sources create updrafts, and a third mechanism where all updrafts carry your hang glider upward. They left it up to players to use these mechanisms together.

Can story be emergent?

A lot of people have talked about creating games with emergent story. *Wildermyth* and *Elsinore*, for example.

But lots of games touted as having emergent narrative do not have it in the emergent gameplay sense. The player can make choices that affect the resulting story. But the resulting story is still something that the narrative team has written.

A truly emergent narrative game would strew narrative elements around the map and let the player make sense of them. Richard Rouse III calls that an "open-ended story."[1] You give the player enough bits of a story that they can find their own meaning, but not so much that you force the player into your interpretation. One player may come away with a very different experience than another.

Narrative elements can mean different things in different order. For example, if a spouse has sex with a third party and then the couple separates, that's one story; if the couple separates and then a spouse has sex with a third party, that's a different story.

Essentially this is what open-ended games (or "toys") like *The Sims* do: allow the player to create characters, name them, give them quirks, and then throw them into a neighborhood where they will do … stuff.

Likewise, Tarn Adams' *Dwarf Fortress*. The dwarves will react to things you do, not always in ways that you intended. (The game's motto is "Losing is fun.") Each playthrough is its own story.

Fortunately for those of us who make a living telling stories, not everyone likes these games.

Why not? Maybe because we want a story to have a point? And stories generated by the chaotic interaction of systems don't have points?

NOTE

1 Richard Rouse III talk at the GDC Narrative Summit of 2016, "Dynamic Stories for Dynamic Games."

CHAPTER 6

Narrative Delivery Systems

Narrative delivery systems are the systems we use to deliver narrative to the player. (Surprise!)

When you tell non-gamers that you write video games, they often assume that you're writing scripts for cinematics, the brief movies you can watch in a game. But cinematics are only one in a fleet of narrative delivery vehicles. Some of them cost a big chunk of the budget. Others cost little more than a writer's time.

GAMEPLAY

Some folks believe that the ideal game narrative consists of only things that happen in gameplay. I'm not that fond of this notion. (Also surprise!) There are lots of stories that cannot be told through gameplay, so you're limiting yourself. So much of human experience involves talking to each other. So little of it is about punching each other in the face.

However, I do believe that the mechanics of a game should relate to the theme and the story. *We Happy Few* is about a few people trying to escape a society where you are forced to pretend that you're happy all the time, while the world spirals down the toilet. We worked on putting "social stealth" mechanics into the game. You wouldn't hide from the other non-player characters (NPCs); you would hide your dark feelings from them. Walking down the street in plain sight was fine, so long as you

DOI: 10.1201/9781003589068-6

waved a cheery "Lovely day for it!" to anyone you passed. Being noticeably off your happy drugs would trigger a mob, but taking your drugs in front of them would pacify them.

Alas, we did not have enough AI programmers, so we didn't accomplish as much of this as we wanted.

We also considered a mechanic where if you overdosed on happy drugs, the procedurally generated map would regenerate. The happy drugs were supposed to induce amnesia; the map changing would feel like your memory was betraying you. We decided that might be incredibly annoying to the player, so we didn't do it.

The *Hit Man* games are similarly about hiding in plain sight, reinforcing the idea of an assassin who is a master of disguise.

Braid allows the player to play with time in order to solve puzzles, in order to rescue the main character's beloved. The story hangs on a major revelation related to its time-bending mechanics. *Octodad*'s ridiculous movement control system makes you feel how hard it must be to be an octopus pretending to be a human dad. *The Stanley Parable* explores tropes as you explore all the different paths your hero can take.

Eternal Darkness: Sanity's Requiem (2002) helps you identify with your character's increasing loss of sanity by messing with the controls and the user interface, and eventually presenting you with a fake game crash where an error message tells you that all your GameCube save files are being deleted.

In *Metal Gear Solid*, a villain called Psycho Mantis shows just how strong his psychic powers are by reading your Playstation's memory card and commenting on the games you like. Then, he dodges and ducks all your attacks, because he can read your mind. In fact, he is almost impossible to beat unless you switch your controller to another port.

It is great if you can make the gameplay part of the narrative. However, most games don't. Not every story lends itself to gameplay, just as not every story makes a good TV show, or comic, or novel, or movie. The list of things we can get video game characters to do is not that long. Supposing that you want to tell a story of a father and a son who don't understand or respect each other, but change their minds over the course of the game. What mechanic could you come up with to gamify that? Or rather, what mechanic could you come up with, that wouldn't feel horribly cumbersome?

For *We Happy Few*, the second playable character, Sally, has a baby which she cannot let anyone else know exists. The baby needs various things to stay alive. What if the player doesn't bother? We didn't want to let the player simply ignore their baby.

I pitched that if you ignore your baby, it would eventually die. I recorded an absolutely heart-wrenching performance by our actress, Charlotte Hope, for this eventuality. My colleagues felt that was too harsh and might make the game not fun.

One of our level designers came up with the idea that if you ignore your baby's needs, you receive an item in your inventory representing the weight of your guilt. Your inventory was limited by weight so that as your guilt increased, which it would, you could carry fewer and fewer useful items. Thus, the player is forced to attend to their child.

Players were not too happy about this. Yes, it was immersive. But some complained that it was … not fun.

I made up a workshop for my narrative team called "Gamify This!" One player pitches something narrative from another medium – ideally, something that does not seem at all amenable to being conveyed by gameplay. For example, the elegiac moment at the end of F. Scott Fitzgerald's novel *The Great Gatsby*:

> Gatsby believed in the green light, the orgiastic future that year by year recedes before us. It eluded us then, but that's no matter—tomorrow we will run faster, stretch out our arms farther.…
>
> And then one fine morning— So we beat on, boats against the current, borne back ceaselessly into the past.

The other players then pitch game mechanics to create the same feeling through gameplay. The fun of the game is to come up with outlandish game mechanics for narratives that really don't lend themselves to gameplay.

Most game narratives cannot be expressed in gameplay, because most stories are about things that a videogame character just can't do. Videogame characters can jump, shoot, and punch. They can woo, in basic ways. But they cannot, in ordinary gameplay, wheedle, mope, or sulk. They cannot be envious. They cannot yearn. Those things require narrative systems to convey.

Also, all too often, a game's narrative isn't even considered until the basic gameplay is nailed down. When I came on board *Contrast*, the shadow mechanics were already pretty far advanced. I could pitch a film noir-style narrative that resonated with them, but the mechanics were not, in and of themselves, telling a story. Likewise, when I came on board *Every Day We Fight* and *Biomorph*, the mechanics were already pretty advanced, and they were not telling a story – though they left lots of room for narrative to tell a story.

And that's fine. I'm pretty happy with the story we told on *Contrast.* And there are many excellent, iconic games where the gameplay and the narrative sleep in separate bedrooms, or only get the player every other week.

So, most game narrative depends on narrative delivery systems other than gameplay. Generally, we just hope that nothing in the gameplay actually *contradicts* the narrative. (Remember "ludo-narrative dissonance"?)

Here are some of those narrative delivery systems, not in order of importance, but mostly in order from most expensive and time consuming to least expensive and quickest.

CINEMATICS

Cinematics are little movies that play from time to time to advance the story. These may be dramatic scenes between characters, or moments of spectacle.

Or they may be rewards for gameplay. Or they may be there to remind the player why they should care about what's going on in gameplay. A dramatic scene may reveal something about the player character's past. It may also change the PC's objective.

A fully voiced and animated dramatic scene is the most powerful way to reveal to the player who the characters are, especially the player character. Many games use dramatic scenes to progress the story, when the mechanics aren't really there to progress the story through gameplay.

Cinematics may be scenes where the player can't be given a choice, because the plot requires they make a mistake or a bad decision, or where the player must not succeed so that the player character can get knocked out and captured.

Cinematics may be sequences of spectacular action where something needs to happen that the game doesn't have mechanics for. For example, the player character getting caught in an avalanche or getting picked up by a giant bird. Or getting rescued from an avalanche by a giant bird.

What is the difference between a dramatic scene and a spectacle? Either may have dialog or no dialog. A dramatic scene is **characters trying non-violently to get something *that the other character doesn't want to give.***

There must be **resistance**. A dramatic scene is about the "play" between the two characters with opposing motivations. The fun of the scene is in what the two characters do to avoid giving each other satisfaction. When either of the characters gets what they want, or realizes they're not going to get it, the scene is over. (Unless realizing they're not going to get it gives them a new objective, which they pivot to.)

Cinematics are expensive. They are usually voiced by professional actors. They have to be animated – either keyframing by hand, which is painstaking, or through motion capture (mocap), which is expensive and still quite painstaking. It can take a single animator a month to animate a scene that the writer took a day to write. Animation is getting cheaper and faster every year, and tools that animate facial expressions and mouth movements are getting more and more powerful. But cinematics are still, in words per dollar, the most expensive narrative delivery system.

Strictly speaking, cinematics do not have to have dialog. If you can communicate the feelings you need to communicate in gestures, music, camera moves, and lighting, God bless us one and all. However, bear in mind that you can't count on the CGI model's subtle acting. Even if you can record a great actor's face using a performance capture rig, you're never going to get cinematic-quality acting from a video game character model. The animators may tell you they can do it, but don't believe them.

(When I say, "never," I mean, of course, "not for at least seven years.")

Cinematics also don't, strictly speaking, have to have voice performances. A low-budget game could just have text on the screen. Basically, any dialog delivery system can be just text on the screen. That's rare in big-budget games these days. It's more for indie games that just don't have the resources to hire actors and audio programmers.

A lot of game designers hate, hate, hate cinematics because they take control away from the player. During a cinematic, the game controls the movements of the characters and the camera. To many game designers, the whole point of a game is that the player has control and can make choices. "It's a game, not a movie," they will say, as if you were not aware of that.

Unless you have a massive budget and the company has the willingness to throw money around, avoid using cinematics for anything that some other narrative delivery system could do. For example, as much as possible, avoid using cinematics for exposition. There are ways to communicate narrative without disabling the player's input, and they're cheaper, too. We don't need to take the controller out of the player's hand in order to tell the player character there's a witch who lives in the house on the top of the hill, and here's how you get up there.

Keep cinematics short. You'd be amazed how much story you can get across in 60 seconds if that's all you've got.

A cinematic doesn't have to be the whole scene. You can start a conversation as a walk-and-talk, then use the cinematic for the critical moment, and then segue into a voiceover.

However, cinematics are the most effective delivery system for emotional scenes, *because* we control every movement the character makes, and exactly where the camera is. We get to take advantage of the past 120 years of cinematic craft.

The opening cinematic, in particular, can quickly define the elements of the story:

a. Who is the main character?

b. What do they want?

c. Why can't they get it?

d. What risk are they running?

e. What do they hope to gain?

It can define the main character's "ghost" – the thing that haunts them. It can establish the historical background in which his story takes place.

And it can make us care.

ANIMATICS

A big step down in expense is animatics. These are a series of still pictures (sketches or lovingly rendered) cut together with live audio.

A really expressive drawing can communicate to the player almost as much as an animation can. Just look at how expressive comic books and graphic novels can be. Plus, an animatic can determine how long we spend looking at each frame. Plus they have sound.

Animatics are much cheaper than cinematics because they contain no animation. However, they can contain camera moves – zooms in and out, tracking shots, crane shots, cuts, dissolves, and fades, all that Ken Burns stuff. Those are easy to make in video editing software such as Adobe Premiere.

A triple-A game team may create an animatic out of the storyboards for a cinematic to test how the cinematic will play in the game. An indie team may just put the animatic in the game.

TABLEAUX VIVANTS AND OTHER HYBRID SYSTEMS

Sometimes, the audio is almost, but not quite, enough to tell the story by itself.

A *tableau vivant* is a sort of in-game diorama. Characters and objects are frozen in time but exist in the game world in 3D. Meanwhile, an audio event plays.

We had very simple tableaux vivants in *We Happy Few.* We had a character, Percy, who was important to the story but did not appear in the game. We needed to create a sense of who he had been without breaking the budget. I wrote, recorded, and edited audio scenes which we then played over 3D "still lifes": maybe a shot of a room in Arthur and Percy's house, or a shot of a fountain. The camera would slowly dolly in to keep the frame interesting; the player had no control.

More ambitiously, we can have tableaux vivants that the player can walk around in.

In Lucas Pope's *Return of the Obra Dinn*, flashbacks play out in full audio splendor while we look at one frozen moment from the event we're hearing – in 1-bit black-and-white pixel art. We can walk around in the scene and look at it from different angles, but nothing moves. A sailor falling from a spar hangs frozen in the air.

Animating those scenes would have been far more scope than Lucas Pope could have managed. But he could make great audio scenes, and build the scenes physically, so long as they didn't move.

It's not surprising that teams often use hybrid systems for flashbacks or dream sequences. They are obviously artificial. Real memories are fully cinematic. No one has a memory where everyone is frozen in time while the audio plays. Using a hybrid system helps convey the strangeness of a dream or the unreliability of a memory.

IN-GAME CONVERSATIONS

Cinematics and animatics are not "in-game" because they are often pre-rendered. The video is animated in-studio, and then the game plays back the pre-recorded video.

STATIC CONVERSATIONS

An in-game conversation may simply be a cheaper and simpler version of a cinematic. Instead of keyframe animating or mo-capping the characters, we pre-program the characters that exist in the game to move in certain ways. We may use animation "loops" – series of movements that repeat. Instead of animating faces or using performance capture (face capture), we may use stock expressions.

Because the characters exist in the game engine, we can allow the player to control the camera. That restricts what we can do to make the conversation powerful, but it may reduce the player's frustration, since they can do something with their hands while the dialog plays. This sort of conversation is more appropriate for exposition, where emotion isn't the point.

The player will often be free to move about normally. *Control* took this approach during expositional scenes, for example. This gets a bit weird when the player character jumps up on a table and the NPC they're talking to doesn't seem bothered by it. But if the player finds that too weird, all they have to do is not jump on a table.

DYNAMIC IN-GAME CONVERSATIONS

An in-game conversation can take place while the character is moving through the environment. A line of dialog may be triggered by entering a certain volume on the map. (A **volume** is a big invisible box in the game world. When the player character enters that box, it triggers the line.)

If the player does not move at the speed we expected, the lines can get spread out oddly – or conversely, may trigger one on top of another. (One thing we can be sure of is that, if there is a way to break a game, players will find it.) The game's dialog system can prevent lines from stacking up on top of each other by holding one line back until the previous line has played.

Alternatively, the whole conversation may be triggered at once, and will then continue to play regardless of whether the player character continues to move or not. *God of War* and *God of War: Ragnarök* take that approach. Kratos often has long conversations with Atreus and other companion NPCs. Sometimes I stop moving along the path so I can focus on what the companion character is saying.

Conversations while moving are not too hard to handle, because the companion is usually either behind or in front of the hero; either way, we can't see their face. We can't see the hero's face either. So, no animation is involved, beyond what moving through the environment already requires.

Conversations while moving can be much longer than cinematics, because the player is already having fun moving. However, we can't put anything key in a moving conversation because the player is only half paying attention to what's being said.

If something in the environment can interrupt a moving conversation, then the game will need a built-in mechanism for interrupting it. We may need lines to cap off the conversation, and lines for resuming it. In *God of War: Ragnarök*, Mimir tells stories on the boat. If the boat hits land, Kratos will say something like, "Enough. We have work to do." The next time you're in the boat, Mimir might resume with, "As I was saying…"

Emotionally powerful conversations can take place between the player character and someone offscreen. *Firewatch* is a series of conversations between the protagonist, and someone he's talking to on the radio.

We used the same technique for *We Happy Few: Roger and James in They Came from Below*. For most of the game, James is just a voice on the radio. But Roger and James are hashing out everything wrong with their relationship while having to deal with robots from another universe, so it gets a bit heated. "Go fuck yourself, Roger. I left everything for you."

This sort of conversation with someone costs practically nothing. We don't see anyone talking, so nothing has to be animated.

These days, games usually don't worry about how the character's physical state would affect their voice. Regardless of whether the player character is moving or still, we use the same vocal performance. However, *Marvel's Spider-Man* had two takes of each line, one for standing still, and one for flying across the city, and folks were delighted. That may become the gold standard in the future, to the cheers of actors and their agents.

BRANCHING CONVERSATIONS

As noted in our "Linear vs. Dynamic Narrative" section, dialog can branch. We can give the player options for what they want their character to say, and different responses for the NPCs talking to them.

Branching conversations can be realized using any delivery system you can use for a linear conversation. The branches may be full cinematics. They can be in-game cutscenes. They can give the characters simple "idles," animation loops that give the impression of a living character without much work for the animators. They can be animatics. They can be still frames, where the other character only changes pose between dialogs. *Banner Saga* takes this approach.

When branching conversations have consequences, they are part of branching narrative, as noted above.

AMBIENT CONVERSATIONS

Conversations don't need to involve the protagonist. They can be between two or more NPCs.

Ambient conversations are **scripted events** usually triggered when the protagonist gets close enough to overhear them. The player can then linger and listen in or keep going on their way.

If the player can interact with any NPC involved in an ambient conversation, either by talking to them or attacking them, then the game needs to provide a convincing way to interrupt the conversation.

Ambient conversations do not need to make sense to the player. In *We Happy Few*, we planned a series of ambient conversations in which you repeatedly heard a punchline ("No, *those* are the nuts!") but you would never get to hear the joke. You know, just like in life.

Ambient conversations are not cheap. Unlike moving conversations, we need to be able to see both characters' faces, which means they have to be animated, usually with canned gestures (loops). However, they are a great way to make the player feel immersed in the world. It would be disappointing if you were in a bustling market, and no one said anything intelligible.

Scripted ambient events don't have to have dialog, of course. In our market scene, we could have a couple smooching. We could have a woman slapping a man in the face and walking off angrily. We could have a cutpurse stealing someone's money. We could have someone walking down the street carefully balancing five clay pots stacked on top of one another. Will he drop them? Let's watch.

The risk in having that scene play silently is that the player may not notice. If the guy is yelling "coming through!" the player is more likely to turn and watch. If someone spent a month animating or programming that little scripted event, we don't want the player to miss it.

SYSTEMIC DIALOG, AKA BARKS

Player characters and NPCs can say certain things when certain conditions are met. E.g., "frag out!" when they're throwing a grenade, or "grenade!" when a grenade is thrown at the player. These are called **barks**. They are **systemic**, in the sense that they are programmed to trigger when certain conditions are met, rather than being scripted to trigger at a certain point on the map. A programmer creates the trigger for barks; a level designer places the trigger for scripted events.

It is generally felt that systemic barks should not "pop" too much – they should not be too memorable – because we'll hear them over and over.

- Tourist!
- Bandit!
- Wrecker!
- Thief!
- Rotten apple!
- Scrounge this!
- Robber!

We went the other way on *We Happy Few.* Some of our barks were memorable (I hope). If you give a bobby (policeman) a bribe, he will say one of these:

- Well, isn't this an unexpected surprise!
- Well, well, well. That's right kind of you.
- I'm right chuffed to know the constabulary is appreciated.
- That's dreadful decent of you!
- We don't get a lot of thanks in the line of duty.
- That is kind of you, sir. Normally ours is a thankless profession.
- I'm touched. Truly.

I've never seen players complain about it.

However, if you do put memorable barks in, there better be a lot of them, or they will get tiresome. "Reloading!" never sounds repetitious. "I love you, little lead slugs!" will wear out its welcome. We chose the riskier "memorable barks" route for *Fragpunk* and found that we needed more than the usual number of dialog lines, because ours stick in players' heads.

For that matter, even if the barks aren't that memorable, more variety is better, especially when they get triggered often.

AUDIO-ONLY

There are lots of narrative delivery systems that are audio-only. Anything audio-only is vastly cheaper than anything audio-plus-visuals. Audio can also be played during gameplay. We don't have to take the controller out of the player's hand.

Audio-Only Conversations

Conversations don't have to be visible, and they're cheaper if they're not. You might overhear a conversation behind a closed door. In *God of War: Ragnarok*, Atreus listens through a door to Sif and Thor arguing about their daughter.

Almost all of the dialog in *Firewatch* is between the protagonist (who you don't see because it's a first-person game) and his offscreen supervisor, who he talks to via walkie-talkie. That was also true for *We Happy Few: Roger*

FIGURE 6.1 The course of true love never did run smooth.

and James in They Came from Below: the two heroes mostly talk over the radio. In *Hellblade 2: Senua's Sacrifice*, the heroine hears voices in her head.

Narration

Narration is someone talking directly to the player from a different time or place than the player character is now. It might be the player character themselves, narrating their own story years later. It might be an NPC who lived through the same events. It might be an unidentified person telling the story of the game to the player. I wrote a game, *Stories: The Path of Destinies*, that's narrated by an unknown person.

Narration tends to emphasize that what happens in the game *is* a story. It can create a literary tone. For instance, "The stabweed hurt like a broken heart" (*Bastion*).

Narration is great for putting the game's events in context, telling us what came before: "There hadn't been dragons in the valley in four hundred years." Or, what will come after: "She would remember that day as the last day of her childhood."

Narration can also tell us things that the player character would never say, or might not even be entirely aware of. "They were being nice to her. That happened so rarely it must be a trick."

A narrator who is an NPC in the game does not have to be reliable. They can relay things the way they see them or just their point of view. *Disco Elysium* is "narrated" by different aspects of the player character's personality. Some of these aspects give hilariously bad advice.

Generally, narration should not be used to tell the player something that they just saw happen. (Remember "show, don't tell"?) It should ideally tell the player something that can only be conveyed by a narrator.

However, that's not a rule. *Bastion* goes hard in the "comment on everything" direction, giving fighting tips, telling the player how long they'll have to fight before something happens, and sometimes just telling – in a literary way – what just happened.

And, of course, *The Stanley Parable* has a hoot with the narrator getting exasperated when the player does not obey his narration.

Self-Talk

Self-talk can either be the character's thoughts or things they actually say. If they're thoughts, they'll be treated differently in audio – everyone's voice sounds deeper and richer inside their own head.

In a third-person 3D game, you might be looking at the player character, but their back is to us, so self-talk is essentially an audio-only narrative system.

Self-talk is common to call out the next step in a series of objectives: "Now all I need is a ladder." Or, to acknowledge picking up an item: "That'll come in handy." Or to tell the player that they're barking up the wrong tree: "I'll never be able to climb this wall!" "I better get going." "I don't need to be here right now." Or to draw attention to something the player might have missed: "Hello, what's this?"

This sort of self-talk can be used as a lazy way to rescue vague level design. If the player has no idea what to do next, instead of giving them a line, it is generally considered better to fix the level so the player can tell for themselves what they're supposed to do next. If you need the player to look up, have something hanging down. They'll probably want to see where it's hanging from.

If the game production has run out of time and there's no time to fix the level, then yes, self-talk can clarify things. But as with any form of hinting to the player, don't overdo it, and try to delay any hints until the player has had time to try to figure things out for themselves.

Self-talk is also useful when the hero has something on their mind that they wouldn't say to the NPC they're talking to.

Sarcastic disbelief: "Yeah, right."

Self-awareness: "I'm sounding crazy, aren't I?"

Self-talk is a cheap, efficient way to remind the player what sort of person the hero is when they are in a long stretch of gameplay.

Systemic Self-Talk aka PC Barks

We can use self-talk barks to communicate the state of the player character in case the player fails to notice something in their HUD (heads-up display). For example, if the player character is low health, or starving, or thirsty, or overburdened, in games where those conditions are relevant. Or bleeding:

- Bloody hell, I'm bleeding!
- That rather hurts, actually.
- I should wrap up that wound!
- Feeling a bit dizzy!
- How am I gonna get this blood out of my clothes?

The UI (user interface) may well throw an icon up on the screen that indicates bleeding, but unless it's blinking, the player may not notice it. (And if it is blinking, it can become annoying quickly.)

Self-talk barks are cheap. Even in a third-person game, we generally don't see the main character's face outside of a cinematic. So they don't require animation.

Self-talk barks are a powerful tool for getting into the player character's mind. We can use it to show how the player character feels about other people. "Oh, great. It's Aunt Margaret. I bet she needs money again." We can use it to establish the main character's backstory. "I wish I'd gone to a high school this nice." We can set a tone. "Creepy!"

In *We Happy Few*, Arthur had a slew of distinctive self-talk barks. For example, when looting someone he'd just killed in combat, he might say, "I actually think you owed me a bit of money," or "That's for knocking down my blocks in kindergarten!" That helped define him as a high-strung, self-justifying anti-hero rather than a typical gruff, laconic video game hero.

He had a big set of random thoughts that would trigger whenever the player was out of combat and standing still for a little while. Many of them were about his autistic brother Percy. Arthur is escaping Wellington Wells to find Percy; the barks help remind the player of this overall objective.

- I should have gone with him.
- I wonder if this is how Percy felt, not fitting in anywhere.
- Of course, Percy never cared much that he didn't fit in. I'm not even sure he knew what fitting in *was*.
- They all said he was dim. He wasn't dim. He was just … strange.
- I wonder if he ever figured it out. Why I wasn't on the train.
- If some scientist had told me Percy was actually from Mars, I'm not sure I'd have disbelieved him.
- Sometimes I wonder, would I even recognize him? He'd be 32 now.… Would he recognize me? Would he want to?
- I wonder if changelings were just what people used to call people like Percy.

- I don't know whether to think about him in the present tense or the past.
- One day we'll all just look back at this and laugh. Ha ha ha. Hah. Heh. Maybe not.
- I miss Mum. Not Dad, really.
- We had a dog, didn't we? When we were very young. Before the War. His name was … Stripe.
- When did it all start to fall apart? It worked for a decade and a half, didn't it?
- It's like I'm living in a fairy tale. One of the horrifying original ones, but in a jacket and tie.
- What did I want to be when I grew up? I can't remember. Isn't that awful?
- Mum never knew what to do about Percy. Except love him. She was good at that.
- It must have been rough on my mum. You don't sign up to have a kid like Percy.
- They never told me what that specialist said, the one in London, when they took him to see him.
- I remember when they came back from London, Mum wouldn't stop crying for a week, but all Percy could talk about was the train.
- If it wasn't for the war, I bet he could have been a great scientist. You don't have to chit-chat to be a scientist.

Repetitive self-talk barks can get annoying if the player feels they don't need them. *Horizon Zero Dawn* suffered from repetitive self-talk barks. There were just too few things for Aloy to say when she picked up something useful. But the player will generally not mind repetitive self-talk barks that are useful to gameplay. "Hmmm, ammo getting low." "I'm starving!"

Self-talk barks are particularly useful when the main character is not a talkative person. How do we know what a laconic, stoic character is feeling? How do we identify with them if we don't know?

They are also useful when the main character is with people they don't trust. There's a lot we think that we don't say. "Can I trust her?" "I need to get away from this guy."

They are also especially useful when the main character is lying. The character can lie to someone and then tell themselves, and us, what they really think.

Audio Logs

Games can convey narrative via recordings that the player is able to trigger. In *Bioshock*, you can find tape cassettes.

In *Horizon Zero Dawn*, you can hear letters and diary entries from people fighting the last war. Once triggered, these keep playing while you continue to explore.

Audio logs are inexpensive – they're just an actor reading a script. AAA games can afford to hire actors to voice 30 or 50 characters, so long as they don't also need character models and animation. Of course, they may not need to hire 30 or 50 actors; many voice actors can do different voices, and so long as you don't hear them in the same 15 minutes, you'd never know it was the same person.

Some players don't care about narratives. Some want as much narrative as possible. Helpfully, audio logs can be **player-pulled**. That is, they don't play until the player chooses to play them. With a player-pulled narrative, the ones who don't care about it don't have to listen to it. The ones who choose to listen to it are more likely to care about it and pay attention to it.

Audio logs don't have to be dialog intentionally recorded by a long-gone NPC. The same mechanism might come across to the player as a ghost whispering to the player when they touch an inspectable spot in the environment or enter a volume or pick up a collectible.

ENVIRONMENTAL NARRATIVE

Chapter 3 discussed environmental narrative and environmental scenarios as good ways to convey the world story. They can, of course, also convey the main story.

In many games, the environment and how it got that was *is* the main story. Why the dinosaurs are robots is part of the Big Secret of *Horizon Zero Dawn*. A similar interrogation of the world is part of the story of *I Was a Teenage Exocolonist* and *Subnautica*.

Any Sherlock Holmes or other detective game is going to have a great deal of investigating the environment, though the game will usually help you interpret what you see.

In *Disco Elysium*, you quickly spot a car that some idiot drove into the canal. The city of Revachol is a decaying mess, so you might think it just means the locals drive badly.

Later on, you discover that you, Harry Du Bois, were the idiot driving the car – and you were blackout drunk. Why you got blackout drunk is key to Harry's personal story arc.

Gone Home is famous as a "walking simulator." It is all environmental scenarios. All you can do is walk around a house looking at things, but by interpreting those things, you put together a whole story about what happened to your missing sister.

Unpacking is not quite a walking simulator – there is gameplay in how you have to take your stuff out of boxes and place them where they go in a series of progressively more grown-up living situations. But the story unfolds as you change homes and put away different things in them.

In *Deus Ex*, Adam Jensen's apartment tells you some of who he is, just as Morgan Yu's does in *Prey.* In *Firewatch*, you return from your walkabout on Day One to discover that your ranger tower has been ransacked.

It is video game developer gospel that the best environmental narrative comes without writing or talking. Sure, graffiti works, and you always need labels on cans and bottles, street signs, and so forth. But what if the scene you've laid out is so evocative that the player can immediately suss out what it says? Isn't that *better?*

You don't need a sign that says, "watch out for icicles!" if you have a pile of broken icicles lying on the sidewalk. And if you show a guy lying there with an icicle speared through his head.

I agree that if a game can say everything it needs to say wordlessly, that's neat. When the player reads something, we are pushing information at them. When they interpret a scene of environmental narrative, they are pulling information out of it, and in turn, pulling themselves into the scene.

And, when the player interprets, they bring their own imagination, which will give them an experience that is fresher and more distinct and unique than anything we can shove at them.

That said, no amount of cleverness in environmental scenarios will tell us what the main character *thinks* about the environment. The guy with the icicle through his head: what does that mean to the player character?

Assuming self-talk is one of the game's mechanics, it can fill us on what the PC thinks: "oh, no, poor guy"? Or, "Oh my God! That's hilarious!" Or, "Goddammit, I warned Uncle Henry to clear off those icicles!"

If you just want the player to have their own reaction to Icicle Guy, you don't need self-talk. If you want the player to know that their character has an unexpected reaction to Icicle Guy, you may need it.

Before writing environmental scenarios, ask yourself what you're trying to convey. Then think of a few different scenarios that could convey that. Then think about which would be simplest to implement in the build. But don't censor yourself too much. The box of toys (or any collection of distinct items) is always going to be a stretch. But artists will have a better idea than you do of what is easiest to make. They will know of hidden difficulties *and* shortcuts. They may also just like one of your scenarios enough that they implement it even though it's a lot of work.

Environmental narrative can be extraordinarily effective. You can tell the player a story through the environment without them even realizing you're telling them anything. It can slip past the player's attention – it's just how the world *is*, so they don't question it the way they might question a dialog scene.

However, it is *not* cheap. Building a model for a car so you can dunk it in the canal is a significant job for an environmental artist. A neon sign may seem simple, but it has to be modeled by an artist. A box full of children's toys is a box full of week-long projects for a modeler. Any art assets will take many iterations to get right.

What is dirt cheap is text.

TEXT

A lot of what you write won't be dialog, it will be prose. Lore is usually prose. Inventories are prose. Descriptions of game mechanics had better be prose.

A lot of what you write won't be dialog, it will be prose. Lore is usually prose. Inventories are prose. Descriptions of game mechanics had better be prose.

Readables

"Readables" are texts the player can collect in the environment that can be read on a separate screen, usually while action in the game is paused. They are usually attached to an interactable object in the game world, but you

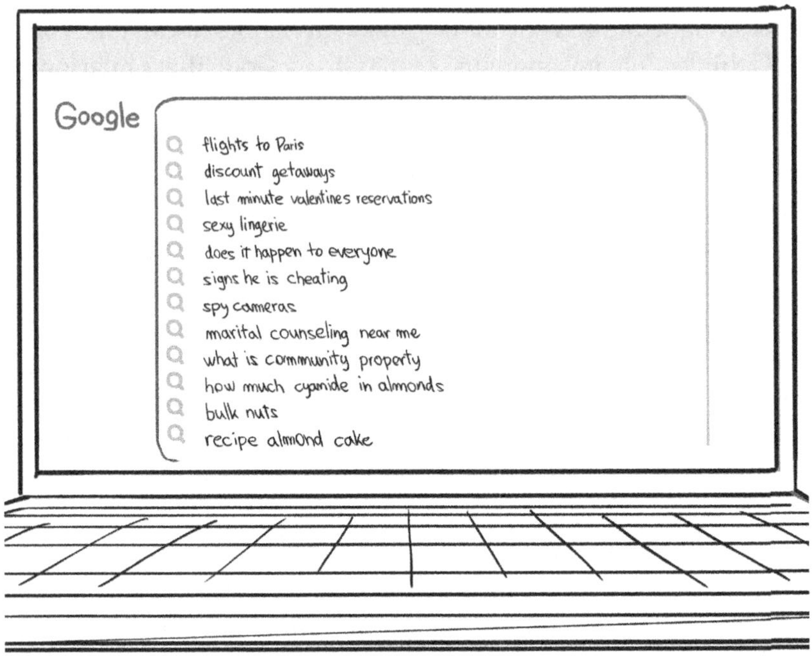

FIGURE 6.2 Every search history tells a story.

can only read the text an inventory screen or a special "Inspect" screen. These might fill out a glossary or codex accessed through the main menu.

If something can be read while walking around in the game world, such as the label on a can, or graffiti on a wall, it's an environmental asset, not a readable as such. The key point of readables is that they do not require distinct art for each item. The text may be in a font; it may appear on a computer screen you can zoom in on. But it's the same computer screen, or scroll, or newspaper, for all the readables in the game. The text is generated from a text file, while the computer screen that you can see walking around does not have legible text.

Therefore, readables are the cheapest way of all to communicate narrative to the player.

They are also probably the least effective. I've heard that only 10% of players bother to read readables. I have no idea if that's accurate. But certainly, we can't depend on the player reading a screenful of text. A lot of people find reading hard, especially if the game is not in their native language. Or they may feel that they didn't play a video game in order to read something. If they wanted to read something, they'd have read a book, wouldn't they? They may be having too much fun playing the game to interrupt gameplay, go to a second screen, and read some text.

That said, many players love readables and will read all of them. In *We Happy Few*, the player could find readable letters in mailboxes. Some of them reveal answers to questions the players might have. To this day, some people are still talking about those letters on forums. They were an easy and inexpensive way to expand and enrich the universe of the game.

Readables are a good task for junior game writers. Readables have few dependencies. They can be put into the game late. Because they usually consist of a text file that is interpreted by a module in the game engine, they are easily edited.

And they don't require a deep understanding of the game medium. Anyone with a talent for putting words together can write a good readable.

Player-Pulled

Narrative delivery systems can be obligatory or optional. Optional delivery systems may be player-pulled or not.

Obligatory delivery systems, just like they sound, can't be avoided. Cinematics that can't be skipped are obligatory. In-game conversations that you must complete before you progress are obligatory. Narration is usually unavoidable, although you can always try to tune it out.

Optional delivery systems can be avoided. If two NPCs are having an ambient conversation, you can listen or walk away. A cinematic that you can skip by holding down "B" is optional.

Player-pulled delivery systems require the player to choose to experience them. If something on the map has an "Interact" button on it, you can choose not to interact with it. You just won't get the narrative triggered by the button. Rarely does a game force you to open a readable. If you don't feel like reading right now, you can pick it up and examine it on your inventory screen later or never.

The benefit of a player-pulled narrative is that it appeals both to people who like narrative and people who don't. People who love reading can go to all the mailboxes in *We Happy Few* and read the letters in them. People who hate reading don't have to. Thus, narrative designers can pack more narrative into these assets, knowing that players who don't care won't feel slowed down by them.

The disadvantage of a player-pulled narrative is that the game story needs to make sense without any of it. Even players who race through the game ignoring letters and cassette tapes and walking away from all the ambient conversations want to know what their objective is and why it's important. If you let them skip important information, the ending may feel unfulfilling, and guess what? They will blame you.

If you don't read all the descriptions of items in Fromsoft's games (*Dark Souls*, *Elden Ring*, etc.) you will miss most of the world-building. You will have no idea what sort of world you're in, except it is obviously not very welcoming. Fromsoft makes demanding games for hard-core players, so it can get away with this. Unless you are making a game for their audience, be careful about hiding everything in the descriptions of weapons.

User Interface Text

Any player-facing text is part of the player experience. When *Dark Souls* throws a huge red YOU DIED on the screen, it tells you what happened in the story (you died) and a bit about how you should feel about it. It contributes to the feeling that *Dark Souls* is a hard-core game. Like the advertising tagline said, "Prepare to die."

After all, a game doesn't have to say YOU DIED. In the *Assassins Creed* games, the game simply informs you that your character has "desynchronized" with their ancestral memory. That makes player character "death" much less alarming and contributes to the generally casual feeling of the AC games. Different strokes.

User interface text is not supposed to have too much flavor. Don't add flourishes. As Winston Churchill said, "Short words are best. The old words when short are best of all."

Weapons, skills, and cards often have a clever name ("Boom Broom"). However, their on-screen descriptions should never sacrifice accuracy or clarity for flavor.

Try to write like you would speak. Avoid 'written' formulations like "teams engage in a best-of-seven battle." If you were explaining that concept to someone in an elevator, you'd probably say, "First team to get to four wins."

Sometimes, in order to be clear and to write like you speak, you need a few more words. For example, "like you speak" is more words than "colloquially." But "write like you speak" is clearer and simpler. Short words are best.

Omit needless words. In "The attacker wins by planting the bomb successfully," you don't need the word "successfully" unless there is a way to plant the bomb unsuccessfully.

Make your sentences as short as possible, but no shorter than possible. Stop trimming when trimming would reduce the amount of information in the sentence.

The best guide to writing clear and concise prose is *The Elements of Style* by Strunk and White. It is super clear and super short. (The best guide to writing *stylish* prose is any detective novel by Raymond Chandler.)

READABLES ARE UNDER THE RADAR

The more expensive a narrative delivery system, the more people will want input on it. Cinematics will go through a slew of approvals. Readables, though: you can generally, within reason, write whatever the hell you want in a readable. They cost almost nothing. No one on the team has time to read them. So you end up with a lot more latitude than you have writing cinematics.

GAMES TITLES

The most important narrative delivery system is the game's title!

At some point, you may be called upon to propose a title for a game. This generally won't happen on a AAA game, where the title belongs to the marketing department, and is probably FranchiseName: Subtitle. On smaller teams, though, it comes up surprisingly often. I've been part of the team coming up with names for *We Happy Few*, *Stories: The Path of Destinies*, *South of Midnight*, *Biomorph*, and *Fragpunk*.

Games usually start with a working title or a code name. *We Happy Few* started as *Glimpse*. *South of Midnight* was *Midnight*. The video game industry is secretive; most companies don't like anyone to know what they're working on.

A working title can inspire people and give them a sense of what sort of game they're working on. *Midnight* is the witching hour, and the game is about a girl with witchy powers; if it had been a more humorous game, we might have codenamed it *Moonshine*. *Glimpse* referred to an early game mechanic where the procedurally generated world would regenerate whenever you weren't looking.

The title needs to be something that players feel good about playing.

It can't be too hard to type. I pushed for our game to be called *I'm Afraid We've Come to the End of Our Time*, but that was perceived as too long. (We eventually made a little spinoff VR game called *We've Come to the End of Our Time*.) Even *Call of Duty* gets abbreviated to COD because 12 letters are too much.

The main purpose of the title is to get people interested in finding out more about the game.

It can, first of all, just tell you what the game is about. *Thief* is about a thief. *Portal* is about making portals. *Civilization* is about building your civilization. *Where in the World is Carmen Sandiego* is about figuring out where Carmen Sandiego is. *Unpacking* is about unpacking. *I Was a Teenage Exocolonist* is about being a teenage exocolonist. Surprise!

More often, the title hints at what the game is about without stating it so baldly. *Deus Ex* is about technologically enhanced human beings. *Deus ex machina* is a phrase meaning "god out of the machine." The main character is part man (in God's image) and part machine.

Kentucky Route Zero is about a road trip through Kentucky. But routes are never numbered zero, and the road you're on isn't normal at all.

Call of Duty is a game about war. "Call of duty" is an old phrase referring to serving as a soldier.

All of these titles suggest rather than saying. A player seeing "Kentucky Route Zero" in the Steam Store will hopefully think, "Huh. What's *that* about?" The rule in marketing is "sell the sizzle, not the steak."

We chose the title *South of Midnight* because the game was set in the South, and it's about a witch, and midnight is the witching hour. But the title was also meant to be mysterious. How can something be South of a time of day? Something is afoot.

We Happy Few ironically suggested that our few townspeople were happy, which indeed they were, but only because they were on happy drugs all the time. There are also fewer and fewer of them. Players could guess that the title was ironic. But how?

Fragpunk is set in a fragmented universe. We threw in the word "punk" for flavor– the tone of the game was brash and irreverent – but then the game designers took that as a cue to get more inspiration from music.

Biomorph is about a critter (a biological) who takes the shape (morph) of other critters.

What sort of a game are you trying to sell people? Is it quirky? Is it a survival game? Call it *Don't Starve*. Is it about an octopus masquerading as a suburban dad? *Octodad*. Is it a dungeon crawler which is also a dating sim? *Boyfriend Dungeon*. A bureaucrat in a depressing Soviet-style transit office? *Papers, Please*.

Of course, a game title can just be plain mysterious. *The Return of the Obra Dinn* is pleasantly ominous.

But a completely mysterious title may not help with marketing. *Disco Elysium* was a hit, but probably not for its title. *Oxenfree? Undertale? Sigma Theory? Umurangi Generation? Engare? Goragoa? Zoombinis?* It's best when the title doesn't just stand out, it gives you at least a hint about the game.

CHAPTER 7

Dirty Narrative

WHAT IS DIRTY NARRATIVE?

Dirty Narrative is a term I made up to describe an approach to writing video game narrative. We used it a lot in *Contrast, We Happy Few*, and the *South of Midnight* alpha.

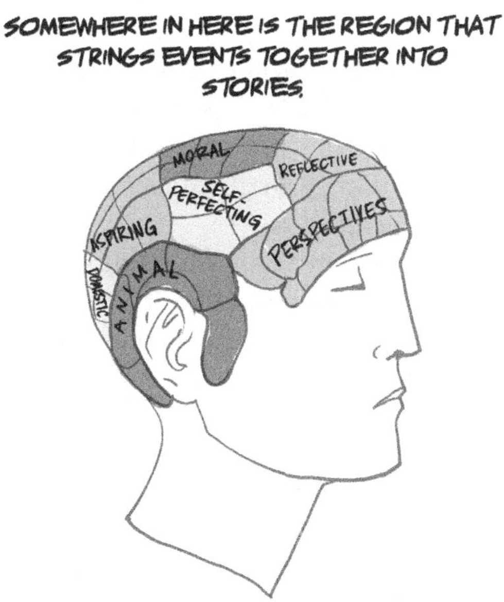

FIGURE 7.1 I believe that we are hardwired to perceive the world through stories.

DOI: 10.1201/9781003589068-7

We are all used to making out the truth from scanty facts. In life, we never have all the information; we have to make educated guesses about what other people are really up to and why. Our brains are hard-wired, I believe, to make up stories about what we can't see out of what we do see.

That's why all great fiction demands participation. Even supposedly passive entertainments – novels, movies, plays – demand that the audience actively interpret the "text" that the writer presents them with.

But most video game narratives are *too* easily understood. We tell the player exactly where to go and what to do. We say the subtext out loud. Almost no one in a game story lies to the player or even tells half-truths.

This is a "push" narrative: we push information at the player.

Unfortunately, pushing narrative at the player tends to push the player out of immersion.

It's more engaging to get the player to ask a question before we answer it. It's better to hint instead of saying. That creates tension; the answer provides release.

That's a "pull" narrative. We give the player hints and let them pull themselves into engagement with the narrative.

Pull is almost always more engaging than push, whether it's a game narrative, a movie, a clickbait listicle, or a poem.

My mistress' eyes are nothing like the sun.

... starts one of Shakespeare's sonnets, and the reader is already wondering, "why are you insulting your girl, dude?"

Dentists hate this one simple trick!

Oh, fine, what is the one trick? Can I stop brushing?

Before you have a dramatic scene in which truths are revealed, make sure that you already want to know what those truths are. Before you release a lot of emotions, make sure you build up suspense about how those emotions might be released.

(Remember when we said good lore either answers questions the player already has, or raises questions the player can answer through gameplay?)

Game developers often ask me for a twist or a surprise. I think twists and surprise are overrated. What you want is suspense. Just ask famous director and serial sexual harasser Alfred Hitchcock:

> There is a difference between "suspense" and "surprise," and yet many pictures confuse the two.

> We are now having a very innocent little chat. Let's suppose that there is a bomb underneath this table between us. Nothing happens, and then all of a sudden, "Boom!" There is an explosion. The public is surprised, but prior to this surprise, it has seen an absolutely ordinary scene, of no special consequence.
>
> Now, let us take a suspense situation. The bomb is underneath the table and the public knows it; they have seen the anarchist place it there. The public is aware the bomb is going to explode at one o'clock and there is a clock in the decor. The public can see that it is a quarter to one. In these conditions, the same innocuous conversation becomes fascinating because the public is participating in the scene. The audience is longing to warn the characters on the screen: "You shouldn't be talking about such trivial matters. There is a bomb beneath you and it is about to explode!"
>
> In the first case we have given the public fifteen seconds of surprise. In the second we have provided them with fifteen minutes of suspense. The conclusion is that whenever possible the public must be informed. Except when the surprise is a twist, that is, when the unexpected ending is, in itself, the highlight of the story.

Dirty narrative is made up of absences, mysteries, misdirections, contradictions, and translucent lies. All of these get the player to ask questions so that if you later reveal the answer, they feel fulfilled.

- Absences: Something missing from the world so obviously that you feel it. Why are there no animals in *Horizon Zero Dawn*? Why are there no children in *We Happy Few?*
- Mysteries: Questions you have to work to answer, or which are never answered. In *Gone Home*, where did my sister go? In *Myst*, who made all these puzzles, and why?
- Misdirections: Use the player's expectations against them. In *Spec Ops: The Line*, all the video game tropes point to the game ending in a climactic boss battle with your nemesis, Col. Konrad. But that's not what happens. So long as what happens is cooler than what they thought was going to happen, players love being surprised.
- Contradictory stories: Non-player characters (NPCs) can disagree with each other, or with physical evidence. In *We Happy Few*, Arthur

and Sally have conflicting versions of the same scenes. Players are still arguing online which one is more true.

- Translucent lies: Lies that not only make clear what the truth is, but also tell you something about the liar. I love these, and *We Happy Few* is built on them. When Uncle Jack tells you that there is definitely enough food, you know, first of all, that there is not enough food; but you also know something about Uncle Jack.

ABSENCES

Let's say you see a bazillion stars in the night sky. But there is a big black circle where there are no stars. You would assume there is something in the sky that's blocking the stars. The Moon, say. Wait. That's no moon!

In Horizon Zero Dawn, there are humans, but there are no wild beasts.

Well, that's not too odd. Lots of games don't have animals. Animals are difficult to model and animate.

But in Horizon Zero Dawn, everywhere you look there are robot dinosaurs.

Now that *is* odd. Why are there robots and no animals? Why dinosaurs? They're difficult to model and animate.

Where did the animals go? What *is* this place?

In We Happy Few, there are no children. That's not odd. Lots of games don't have children. Children are difficult to model. They come in all different sizes! And people make such a fuss when the player murders them.

But there is an absence where children could be. In Wellington Wells, there are playgrounds, but adults use them. There are child-sized beds, with odd puppets tucked under the covers. In the train station, there is a very old uneaten birthday cake with a birthday card for a boy turning 11.

This is not a typical video game world where the children exist, they're just not around at the moment. There were children. But they are gone. They are *absent*.

Where are the children?

What happened to them?

Once we've got the player to wonder that, we start to answer it. The town of Wellington Wells was occupied by the Germans during an alternate history of World War II. The children were all taken away as hostages.

No one in town talks about the Very Bad Thing. But all of them are racked with guilt. They wear happy masks and take happy pills that make you forgetful, and they get homicidal if you're not taking happy forgetful pills, too.

MYSTERIES

A mystery is a question you don't know the answer to. More: a question you have *no idea* what the answer might be. More: an unanswered question whose answer you are sure is very important.

What comes after life? is a mystery.

Why am I here? is a mystery.

What even are marshmallows? may seem like a mystery, but it is really just a question. Sugar, probably. And some kind of gluey white stuff. I dunno, maybe eggs?

In *Gone Home*, the player character goes home, but her sister's gone, along with everyone else. What happened to her?

What is the deal with the house in *What Remains of Edith Finch*?

Who made the puzzles on the island in *Myst*?

What killed everyone on board the ship in *The Return of the Obra Dinn*?

Most video games resolve their mysteries sooner or later. The games I just mentioned all do; finding out the answers is part of the gameplay. Or, in the case of *Obra Dinn* and *Gone Home*, it *is* the gameplay.

You don't have to resolve mysteries. You can, but mysteries are fun. You should only resolve a mystery when the resolution is more engaging than the mystery itself.

(A liberating discovery I made was that David Bowie's lyrics don't necessarily come out of attempting to make a specific point, but taking words about a subject, cutting them up, and moving them around. "[I] f if you put three or four dissociated ideas together and create awkward relationships with them, the unconscious intelligence that comes from those pairings is really quite startling sometimes, quite provocative." Trying to decipher what he means is beside the point. The mystery *is* the point.)

When folks tell me "I want to know where the kids in Wellington Wells are now," my favorite response is, "Oh, good!"

After all, life is full of unresolved mysteries. That's part of the fun of it.

MISLEADS

When the game tells the player that it is headed in one direction, but it's really not.

The Sixth Sense is a classic movie with a mislead. One of the characters is not what you think he is. He is not even what he thinks he is.

In the pilot episode of *Buffy: the Vampire Slayer*, a guy breaks into the school at night with a girl. The girl is worried that it's dangerous. There are shadows and strange sounds. The guy seems creepy. He keeps reassuring her that she'll be fine. The girl is the vampire.

In *Heavy Rain*, there is something important that you do not know about Scott Shelby, the detective you play. The revelation requires you to reevaluate everything you know about him and everything you did *as* him.

In *Spec Ops: The Line*, the game is not about what it pretends to be about at the beginning.

In *We Happy Few: Lightbearer*, hapless rockstar Nick Lightbearer wakes up covered in blood, with a dead girl in his bed, and ominous lyrics about a killing. He discovers that the lyrics match the scene of the crime. But he can't remember the night before. He doesn't know if he's the killer or not. But after the second and third victims, he's pretty sure he is.

So are the players, because the first two acts of the DLC are about what a horrible person Nick has been to everyone around him. We play the story as the point of it is discovering that he is not just a selfish person but a homicidal maniac, and how does he deal with that?

That is not what he actually discovers. And his story leads to an entirely different revelation.

The key to a good misdirect is that the storyteller commits to it. (See "schmuck-baiting" above.) If you are not wholehearted in your commitment to the fake direction, the audience will suss it out. They'll think what you're doing is clever, but it won't really make them reevaluate anything. To blindside them good and proper, all the levels have to be designed, all the objectives written, as if you are really going off in the false direction.

Say our player character is going home scared because the Big Bad is chasing her. The mislead is that the Big Bad is not only already at her home, but will be an ally.

We need to use every cheesy suspense technique to convince the player she's in danger. So not just tense music and movements in the shadows. Have the heroine walk into a large empty room with health potions and ammo scattered everywhere. Lock the door and autosave. Even contrive for your heroine to be low on hit points, or suffering from a debuff, just so that the player will be worrying about the upcoming fight with the Big Bad.

If we don't use the tropes, the player will know, at some level, that we're not going to go through with it.

You can do misleads in real time, too. We did open development for *We Happy Few*, which meant that as we built the game, we had a lot of people speculating about who the second playable character would be. They were starting to guess that it was Sally, the old flame of the first player character, Arthur.

Well, we couldn't have that. We wanted the unveiling of Sally to be a surprise.

We weren't showing any of the story in Early Access, so all we had to play with was environmental narrative. So, we used environmental narrative to build up a minor character from the introduction, Prudence Holmes. We built an entire offscreen story about Pru escaping Wellington Wells ahead of Arthur, just to throw people off Sally.

CONFLICTING NARRATIVES

In video games, we work hard to make sure all of the facts we present to the player add up to a single coherent vision. We get bug reports about inconsistencies.

What if we embrace conflicting narratives?

Real people contradict each other all the time – even when we're looking at the same thing. Eyewitnesses are notoriously unreliable. People forget what happened, and then reconstruct another version of events, which becomes indistinguishable from a memory in the brain.

Film has taken this on. The classic Akira Kurosawa film *Rashomon* is the trope namer. A rape and murder are recounted five times, five different ways. Which is the truth? We never know, though the last one is the most embarrassing to everyone, so it's probably the closest.

Conflicting narratives ask the audience or player to figure out what the truth is. And that requires paying a lot closer attention to the world than someone who has the truth handed to them. It requires the players to interpret what they see.

In *Narcosis* (2017), the narrator seems to be the player, but things don't quite add up, and it turns out he is someone else entirely.

In *Tell Me Why* (2020), the twins try to uncover what happened the night their mother died long ago. They sometimes remember things differently, and it's up to the player to infer the truth.

In *The Void* (2008), characters lie to you constantly, sometimes for their own agendas, sometimes in the hopes it will help you.

Digital artist Alexander Howard wrote me to add:

> The unreliable narration in the *Zero Escape* games is partially metatextual in places, as in, the player is representing the psychic field and the distillation of ideas through it. In experiencing other timelines, we literally bring them knowledge they shouldn't have.... In *Zero Time Dilemma* [2016], you're also cycling through three playable characters. But there's a *lot* of false information, a lot of player characters remembering things wrong....
>
> *428: Shibuya Scramble* [2008] is another excellent example. It's told by five people who all interact with each other and influence each other's timelines. It's a visual novel where every individual character's route is very introspective and tinged heavily by their own worldview. Some are more objective than others, some are more or less observant, and they all have varying levels of unreliability. For example, the longer I spent with [name of character], the more I realized he wasn't the bad person he was so convinced he was.[1]

There are various twists available for unreliable narrators. In *Disco Elysium* (2019), the various aspects of your personality narrate what's happening, putting different interpretations on what just happened and what it means.

In *The Stanley Parable* (2013), the narrator says what you're going to do before you do it. You can then frustrate him by not following his narration. Both he and the game react entertainingly to your obstinacy.

In the *Dragon Age* franchise, the lore is contradictory and depends on which group's lore you're reading. David Gaider:

> In general, the further the history goes back, we always would purposefully obfuscate it more and more [...] make it more biased and more untrue no matter who was talking, just so that the absolute truth was rarely knowable. I like that idea from a world standpoint, that the player always has to wonder and bring their own beliefs to it.[2]

In *We Happy Few* (2018), our first playable character, Arthur Hastings, has had a crush on Sally Boyle since they were kids. They were the "Two Musketeers." Then one night she ran off and he never saw her again.

They have three scenes together; we see each scene twice, once in each of their playthroughs.

The thing is, in Arthur's versions of the scenes, Sally is written as a lovable, adorable flake who makes outrageous demands for whimsical reasons. In Sally's scenes, she has very solid reasons for all the things she asks for, and Arthur is a selfish jerk.

In Sally's playthrough, Sally tells Arthur a very important thing that he callously ignores. In Arthur's playthrough, she does not say the thing at all.

Did she say it? Did she say it and he blocked it out of his memory? Did she never get the guts to actually say it out loud, and she only remembered saying it? Up to you to interpret.

TRANSLUCENT LIES

It's a conceit in a lot of video games that you can trust anything anyone tells you. NPCs are always filling you in on quests you can go do and what you'll need to complete them. Often, the only NPC who lies is the villain, and he only gets one lie, which is revealed soon enough.

In more advanced narratives, you get people lying to you. But they lie transparently. You can tell they're lying; they're there to lie to you. The bombastic propaganda in Bioshock and Outer Worlds, for example.

A translucent lie is a lie through which you can see the truth, but which also tells you something about the liar.

In *Detroit: Become Human*, an android-hating human named Todd tells you that androids have ruined his life. It's a vague lie, but pretty obviously the lie of someone who blames everyone else for his own problems. And that's the point: the lie tells you all you need to know about Todd. In fact, you really couldn't have Todd be honest about why he is where he is, because then he'd be someone who can face up to his own shortcomings. You need the translucent lie.

The Bloody Baron in *Witcher 3*. He says he's very worried about his wife and sends Geralt off to find her. He claims to know nothing about the fight in his wife's room or why his wife is gone.

His shifty eyes and ashamed glance away as he's saying that tip you off that he's probably lying. And so we're pulled in – what is the lie and what is he ashamed of?

As Geralt discovers, the truth is he was abusive, and the mother and daughter fled. Geralt confronts the Baron.

Now we get the payoff of the lie. He's ashamed of himself. Not for being abusive – for not being able to control his wife and daughter. That's the measure of the man.

We wouldn't get the full sense of the man if he was truthful from the get-go. A man of wounded pride will not tell you his shame up front. To tell his story immersively, we need to start to suspect he's lying and wonder what the truth is and why he wants to lie.

In We Happy Few we have Johnny Bolton. Johnny is a middle-aged man who pretends to be an 8-year-old boy pretending to be a special agent with his dolls. He is very anxious for you to sneak into the secret lair of the evil Dr. Verloc, who is his arch nemesis.

At first, you think this is all a fantasy, that is, a lie. But later you discover that there *is* a Dr. Verloc. He is the scientist in charge of Haworth Labs, which makes all the Joy pills that keep people happy. Except that some of his pills make people utterly crazy.

That's when you start to suspect that this is not *all* fantasy. People rarely lie 100% either. You might start to wonder if Johnny hates Dr. Verloc because Dr. Verloc made him crazy. You might be right.

In *Contrast*, Didi's father, Johnny, keeps telling people, "You think I can't pay you? Look at this suit!" You can guess he's lying and suspect that might be because he spent all his money on that suit.

But Johnny's inept lie also tells you how much Johnny cares about appearances – a guy in a nice suit can't be poor! – and how gullible he himself is.

UNRELIABLE NARRATORS

Absences, mysteries, misleads, conflicting narratives, and translucent lies are all refinements of the general concept of the unreliable narrator.

Human beings carry around a big fancy interpretive apparatus. We don't want to accept facts; we want to interpret them. We *want* to interpret them.

In fact, if you tell people the truth too baldly, and you don't give them a convincing emotional story to go with it, a lot of people will figure you must be lying. They will go searching for the "real" truth. A lot of people will trust someone who says you're lying, based on no evidence at all, just so they can feel smart.

That's why people trust podcasters over thousands of scientists. They don't want to be spoon-fed. They want to feel they sussed out the truth. They don't trust anything they didn't work for.

(To get even further into the weeds, truth without emotion is inherently suspect. In Capgras Syndrome, someone thinks that their wife, say, is an imposter. The theory is that for medical reasons, their emotions about her have become disconnected from their perception of her. Normally they would expect to feel a certain way about her. If they're not feeling that, she must not be their real wife.)

So, an unreliable narrator is inherently interesting – *if* we can see through the narrator to get a sense of what the truth is – and weirdly more to be trusted than a straightforward one.

But isn't dirty narrative risky? What if people don't realize you're doing it? What if they think you're just being sloppy?

Sure, it's risky. We have to make sure the player knows that it's unreliable intentionally, not just because of sloppy writing.

In *We Happy Few,* Sally and Arthur's scenes take place in entirely different places. Partly that was for player agency. We wanted the player to have to earn the scenes. Arthur could come to Sally's house in his playthrough because that was a difficult mission. But he couldn't come to Sally's house in Sally's playthrough, or she'd get the scene without having to do anything. So in her story, she had to meet him in the abandoned Garden District.

But we also figured that players couldn't possibly fail to notice that the same scene takes place in different locations. And surely we were not so stupid to have done that accidentally. We hoped they would draw the conclusion that Sally and Arthur remember things differently. (They did.) We hoped that they would therefore be more likely to pay attention to the other differences in the scenes. (They did.)

So why go to all that trouble?

Making a convincing world is not easy, because the real world has bazillions of elements, while your fellow devs have to painstakingly create every single object, every gesture, every behavior in the world. And obviously, they need to keep things as simple as possible. So video games only

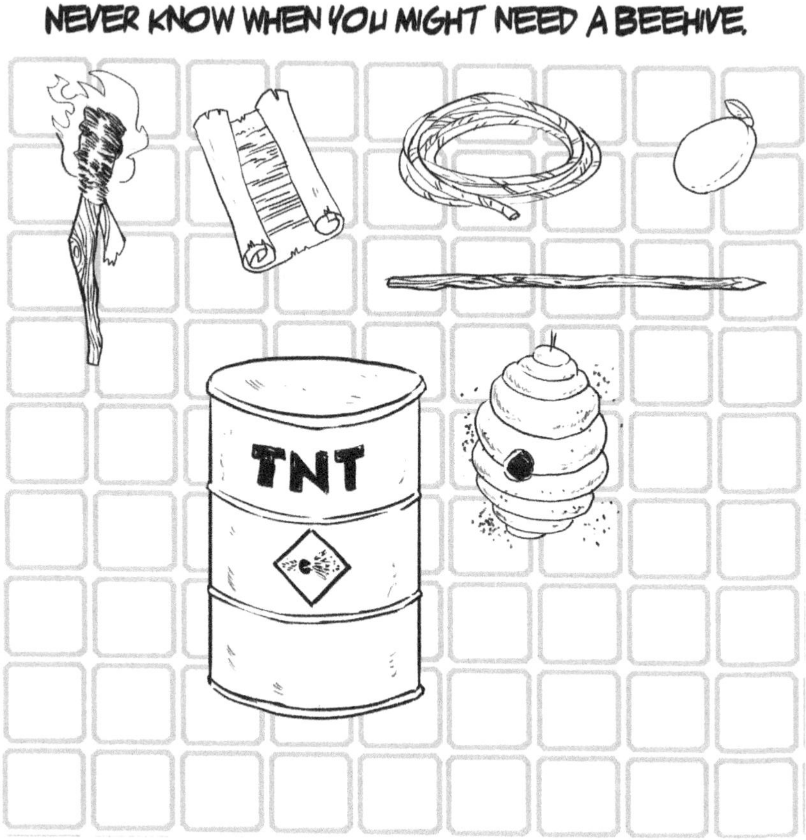

FIGURE 7.2 What has it got in its pocketses?

have thousands of items in them. In other words, video game worlds are *extraordinarily sparse.*

How do we bridge the gap?

We have to make the player fill in our world for us.

Fortunately, all human beings are good at making stories out of limited facts. It saved our lives when we were all hanging out in Africa. We'd be walking through the forest when everything went quiet. And we'd think, "Huh. Just like what Uncle Og said happened just before the lion attacked him!" So we'd be ready for the lion. Human beings who didn't do that got eaten.

By encouraging the players to interpret the world's absences, mysteries, contradictions, and lies, dirty narrative encourages them to work harder than usual to fill in the gaps between things. And that makes the world feel bigger and busier than we can see.

Counterintuitively, when every question is answered and every mystery is explained, our fictional world can feel small. But when there is friction from competing facts, the player extrapolates a richer, more convincing world inside their head than we can ever build inside a computer.

Reality has a shape, and its shape is … asymmetrical. It would be reassuring if the Earth was the center of the universe, but apparently it is not. It is one of many planets orbiting an ordinary class M star off in one of the arms of the Milky Way galaxy.

Reality is made of temporary solutions that got potch keyed on top of other temporary solutions, and now everything's all stuck together, and nothing can be fixed. Reality is not the game you designed, it's the game you shipped.

So if you want to create a reality, don't design a fish. A fish makes too much sense. Someone could have intentionally designed a fish. Instead, design a platypus.

To create a convincing world, you need to create a layer of asymmetry. Of cruft.

When I was at Yale, I took a course on the Afro-Atlantic tradition. Of all the courses I ever took, this one, which had nothing to do with screenwriting, taught me the most about screenwriting.

In West African drumming, I learned that you don't play the beat. You play around the beat. In West African textiles, you don't make a perfectly symmetrical quilt. At least one of the squares is off-center. Or different.

Our game worlds tend to go in the opposite direction. Everything is a little too symmetrical. Too relevant to the main character. Monsters hang around for you to kill them. Quest givers wait around to give you a quest. The player is the center of the solar system.

But when players meet a world that is too neat, too simple, and too symmetrical, they call shenanigans. So give the game world life that has nothing to do with the player. Rumple the beds so they look slept in. Allow the player to be the center of the story, but never of the world.

NOTES

1 https://www.reddit.com/r/wehappyfew/comments/1cafrm1/other_games_with_unreliable_narrators/.
2 https://www.rockpapershotgun.com/the-trick-to-dragon-ages-lore-is-that-the-lore-is-lying-says-original-uber-plot-writer-david-gaider.

CHAPTER 8

Dialog

DIALOG IS HOW WE REMEMBER PEOPLE TALKING

Writing dialog in any medium is tricky. You don't want to write the way people actually talk. If you've ever transcribed an interview, real talk is full of ums, haws, kindas, and repetitions.

Funnily enough, when you remember a conversation, you don't remember the repetitions or verbal tics, unless they are particularly memorable: "Life, uh, finds a way."

Jim Lovell *said*, "Okay, Houston, we've had a problem here." People *remembered* "Houston, we have a problem."

Dramatic dialog should sound or read like what we *remember* someone saying: condensed, focused, even witty. If you were recounting it to a third party, how would you phrase it?

DIALOG IS NOT LOGICAL

Dialog does not have to be logical. Real people regularly respond to all sorts of things that are not what the other person just said. Sometimes they are responding to what they think the other person means to say.

```
                    Alex
      Do we have any cauliflower?

                    Lisa
      Don't we have to go somewhere
      tonight?
```


DOI: 10.1201/9781003589068-8

... because she is assuming that I want to go grocery shopping tonight.

They may respond to what they're scared they'll say, or what they wanted them to say.

Sometimes people are literally just waiting for the other person to stop talking so they can say the thing *they* wanted to say. You can convey a lot of information in a scene where two people are talking past each other.

Sometimes, what the other person said a few couplets back finally sinks in.

```
                 BOB
Red or white?

                ALICE
I'll just have soda water.

                 BOB
Red would go with this steak.

                ALICE
It smells great.

                 BOB
Wait. Soda w-- ? Are you--?
Are we--?
```

If it's not critical for the player to know that Alice is avoiding alcohol because she's pregnant, we can leave it at that. Or we can let it sink in for a moment or two, so the people who figured it out get to feel smart and then clear it up for everyone else:

```
                 BOB
We're pregnant? Is it a boy
or a girl?

                ALICE
          (affectionately)
Idiot. I only just peed on
the stick.
```

You might think that illogical dialog would be hard to understand. But we're all highly skilled at it. We get a lot of practice. Making the player work just a little bit to understand the subtext of what the characters are saying increases immersion and pulls them into engagement with the narrative.

ONE IDEA PER LINE?

Think about how the player is going to absorb your dialog. Consider not giving them too much to absorb in one go. Have a character say a thing, let the other character react, and then have your character say their next thing.

```
              NICE BANDIT
He just wanted to keep his
shoes, man! They weren't even
good shoes!

              MEAN BANDIT
So what? I didn't like his
attitude.
```

That's two ideas in each line. It doesn't seem like a lot to absorb, but the player is probably only going to pick up on one idea per line.

```
              NICE BANDIT
He just wanted to keep his
shoes, man!

              MEAN BANDIT
So what?

              NICE BANDIT
They weren't even good shoes!

              MEAN BANDIT
I didn't like his attitude.
```

This way, the player can absorb each idea on its own.

Incidentally, that's also a good way to write any kind of expository prose: one idea at a time. It's the difference between wolfing a cheeseburger and eating a steak with a fork and knife. A cheeseburger is a lovely thing, but it is a maelstrom of tastes. You can't really taste the cheese or the beef. Mostly, you taste "cheeseburger."

If you have your steak on a plate and you can cut it up into bite-sized chunks, you're going to taste the steak, and appreciate how nicely seared it is, and then taste the green beans, and appreciate how fresh they are.

That doesn't mean your lines can't have layers. Each line can build on the next to create subtext or build a theme. But you may want to feed the information to the player bite by bite.

One idea per line also helps you cut lines that only dilute the argument. All you really need is:

```
                NICE BANDIT
He just wanted to keep his
shoes, man!

                MEAN BANDIT
 I didn't like his attitude.
```

CHEESEBURGERS ARE GOOD, TOO

One idea per line is great for introducing ideas. When you want to create a feeling, sometimes you want poetry: a lot of words that add up to a feeling. Sometimes you want a maelstrom or a flood:

```
                Rick
Inside of us, we both know
you belong with Victor.
You're part of his work, the
thing that keeps him going.
If that plane leaves the
ground and you're not with
him, you'll regret it. Maybe
not today. Maybe not
tomorrow, but soon, and for
the rest of your life.

                ILSA
But what about us?

                RICK
We'll always have Paris.
```

PUSH TEXT INTO SUBTEXT

You don't have to get all that into your dialog in one pass. Start by writing just the text of the scene – who wants what, why they can't get it.

Then do a pass for character revelation. Ideally, each line not only develops the dramatic conflict further, it also reveals something about the character saying it.

Then push the text into subtext. Sure, you can have characters say exactly what they mean (text). But the scene won't be that engaging.

An obvious, on-the-nose scene, where everyone's shouting their feelings, paradoxically engages very little of the player's feelings. Push storytelling pushes the player out of engagement. The more the player has to work at understanding what's really going on in a conversation (subtext) – so long as they do understand it – the more they get emotionally involved in what's happening in the drama.

In jazz, the soloist doesn't play the beat. They play around the beat. The audience knows the beat, so they don't need it restated. Your scene can play *around* the beat.

Characters don't need to ask outright for what they want. It's fun when we leave the player at least some interpreting to do. In real life, we say, "Are you going to finish that" when we mean, "Can I eat the rest of your sandwich?"

They may not even *know* what they want. A character may be asking for a helmet, but we realize that what they really want is permission or forgiveness. They may be asking for an auto part, but what they want is to be treated as an equal.

The art of writing a scene obliquely is giving the player enough clues that they can figure out what's really being asked for. Players love to feel smart!

PHRASING

Another pass can get into the exact phrasing of the dialog. Everyone knows that a character shouldn't say things out of character – that someone like them would never say. But ideally, a character says things that *only they could say.*

Can you look at the dialog without the names attached and know which character is speaking?

Would an actor love to play this part? If not, what would make the part worth playing?

In screenplay format, parentheticals appear below the character name and above the dialog line, in between parentheses. In a spreadsheet, they appear in their own column. They tell the actor how to say the line.

Put statements about feelings into parentheticals, if needed. Avoid writing:

```
                JOSE
      I'm angry! You ate my slider!
```

Real people almost never name their feelings like this, unless they've had a lot of marital therapy. Put it into the parenthetical:

```
                JOSE
            (hangry)
      You ate my slider!
```

Parentheticals allow the performance to contradict how the line is written:

```
                JOSE
          (mock horrified)
     You ate my slider. You--
     monster!
```

Note that screenwriting books, including mine, will tell you to minimize parentheticals, along with camera movements, action description, and location description. That is the usual advice for a selling script (though even there, you may need to ignore it). Ignore that advice when you're writing for a game. Many of the people who will read it do not know how to interpret written dialog. It hurts no one if you specify the emotion for a line if you're unsure it's clear from how the line's written.

READ IT OUT LOUD

Read your lines out loud. Dialog that looks fine on the page may turn out to be complicated or awkward when you try to say it. As Harrison Ford allegedly told George Lucas, "You can type this shit, George. But you sure can't say it."

Even better, if you have a willing accomplice, read the scene out loud between the two of you.

Before getting into a recording studio, it's a good idea to hold a "table read" of all the scripts you have, so everyone can hear the characters' voices. You'll want real actors, though they don't have to be the actors you'll hire for the game itself. You can do the table read over Zoom so that you can record it, and potentially use the recording to turn storyboards into an animatic for devs to watch. Good storyboards, with decent acting, can go a long way to help non-writers understand what the scene is going to sound like in the game.

SAY SOMETHING ONCE, WHY SAY IT AGAIN?

Dialog should not repeat things the player already knows. If the player saw something happen, don't have someone describe it later. If a character absolutely needs to convey something that happened to someone new, you can use cinematic tricks to avoid making the player sit through the recap. For example, cut to a long shot where we just see the two characters talking. Or fade out and fade in. Or start the character recounting the events and then cut to somewhere else, sometime later.

An exception is when you can add a point of view to the recap. For example, if the character is really mad about what happened, or thinks it's hilarious. Or they're going to lie about what happened.

(The writers of the TV series *Rome* made a brilliant choice when it was time for Marc Anthony to give his famous oration on Caesar's death. It's an obligatory scene; you can't skip it. But they knew they were never going to top "Friends, Romans, Countrymen. I come to bury Caesar, not to praise him." So they have a character in a pub *recount* what it was like listening to that speech. And the character didn't even hear Marc Anthony's speech. He was in the back of the crowd. He just saw what Marc Anthony did with Caesar's bloody toga. We hear, not the speech, but how the crowd reacted to the speech. Which, in that series, is the story.)

OMIT NEEDLESS WORDS

Trim your dialog ruthlessly. Often the first sentence you write in a block of text can go. It's general, and the rest of the text is specific. For example:

```
               HERO
You don't know me.

          INTIMATE OPPONENT
I know more than you think.
You used to be a hero, but
something hurt you. Now you're
keeping your head down....
```

You don't need "I know more than you think." You can jump right into the intimate opponent showing that she knows more than the hero thinks.

```
               HERO
You don't know me.

          INTIMATE OPPONENT
You used to be a hero, but
something hurt you. Now
you're keeping your head
down....
```

I can often skip a sentence responding to the previous character's line, and just jump to the second character's point of view.

```
                    SIDEKICK
          You said it was gonna be
          easy!

                      HERO
          I said it was gonna be
          simple.
```

You don't need "No, I didn't" or "I never said that." It's clear from "I said it was gonna be simple" that the hero doesn't agree.

You may need to use italics or underlining so the reader reads the sentence properly. "I said it was gonna be *simple*." Nothing wrong with using italics to make meaning plain. That's why we have italics.

Avoid "As you know, Bob" dialog.

```
                      JOE
          Bob, we've been friends for
          20 years. I used to work in
          the same mines as you,
          remember? Until that injury.
          You remember my injury, don't
          you, Bob? When that soda
          machine fell on my foot?
```

However, you can sometimes take the curse off of this by turning it into an argument.

```
                      JOE
          Bob, how long have we been
          friends, twenty years? Didja
          forget why I don't work in
          the mines any more? Or do you
          just not care?
```

GAME DIALOG IS NOT MOVIE DIALOG

Note that game dialog is not movie dialog. Movie dialog can be quite sparse. That's because great movie actors can convey a lot in silence. They are movie actors because their faces tell us what they are feeling even when they're not saying anything.

There are great voice actors in games. They can convey a lot with how they deliver their lines. But even the best video game actors can't convey that much in the silence. That's because they, themselves, are not on screen. A CGI model is on screen. Even when we do performance capture, putting a camera close to the actor's face, their performance is limited by how much data the p-capture rig can obtain. And that is nowhere near the amount of data that a live human being's face conveys, especially 10 meters tall on a screen in an actual movie theater.

At least not until p-capture and CGI rigs get a lot better. As of this writing, the most impressive video game model performances still read a little dead visually, especially when the character is not talking.

What this means for writers is that you can't write sparse, movie-style dialog. The silences will *not* speak for themselves. Think of game writing as writing dialog for radio. If something emotional needs to be conveyed, it has to be conveyed in words. The actor will need words to speak so that he can act with them; his face will not do the job. Make sure that you've given the actor enough lines that they can work their magic.

PERIOD DIALOG

Ancient people did not speak "forsoothly." That is, they did not sound archaic to each other. They spoke in the very latest, most up-to-date version of their language. Even Ancient Greeks spoke the very latest, most up-to-date Greek. It only became "ancient" after they'd been dead a few hundred years.

Some video games have characters "thee" and "thou" each other. That sounds archaic. Have them talk like they don't know they're living in the past. Because they're not.

That doesn't mean they should use the latest Internet slang, especially since any meme you use will be horribly dated by the time the game comes out. They probably shouldn't say "noob." But they should say "can't" and "won't" and interrupt each other. They can be sarcastic. They can be flirty.

Make them talk like *people*.

INTERLOCUTORS

The main character of a game may not be the ideal person to communicate what is going on with them. A main character may be a man of few words. They may be a liar. They may be a guarded person in a situation where they really shouldn't tell anyone what they're thinking or feeling. They may have gotten blackout drunk the night before and can't remember who they are or what they do for a living.

In that case, we can give the player character one or more **interlocutors**. That's a fancy word for someone to talk to. They don't have to be a sidekick; they can be anyone who meets with the player often.

Where your hero is terse, your interlocutor likes to talk. Where your hero is stoic, your interlocutor expresses all his feelings, including the embarrassing ones.

Your interlocutor can ask what the plan is, and what the plan is when *that* plan goes horribly wrong. They can ask why your hero is refusing the perfectly reasonable-sounding deal that your opponent just offered. They can simply wonder why all of this is happening to them.

They can be a conscience. In *Spec Ops: The Line*, when protagonist Capt. Martin Walker insists that the team has to finish the mission, they have no choice, squadmate Lt. Adams insists, "you always have a choice, man!"

In our final DLC for *We Happy Few*, early versions of Victoria Byng were stoic and guarded, and I found her boring to write. Not good: if you're bored, players will be bored, too.

We decided to have her mother appear to her regularly. Not her real mother, but the version of her mother she kept in her head. (You may have one of these, too.) So we could have scenes of Victoria attempting to justify her actions to her very skeptical mother. We could reveal Victoria's shock as her father began to reveal who he really was, and we could understand the sacrifice Victoria had to make, even though Victoria wouldn't have talked about those things to anyone actually living in her world.

We could have done all that in self-talk, but she would have sounded long-winded and insane. Sober, sane people don't normally talk to themselves out loud at length. Soliloquies are not real life.

An interlocutor can straight up speak the hero's truth. They can say, "You're pretending to be strong, but I can tell you're hurting." They can say, "You keep talking about doing your duty, but you're really just getting back at so-and-so, aren't you?" Very handy when your main character is not aware of his own emotions or is too stoic to talk about them.

If your hero won't talk, go to the store and buy them an interlocutor!

BRANCHING DIALOG

Dialog can branch in the same way that the story can branch. We use similar charts for both – the gauntlet and the branch-and-merge. Both story and dialog branching means lots of index cards up on the wall, or onscreen. But branching dialog doesn't *necessarily* mean the game story branches.

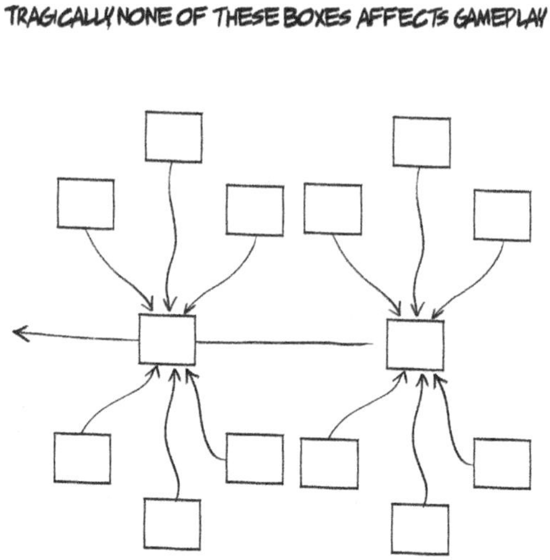

FIGURE 8.1 Hub and spoke.

In a lot of games, dialog has no effect at all on the story. In a typical dialog with a quest-giving non-player character (NPC), the quest triggers regardless of what you say. The game puts all the information necessary for completing the quest in the player's journal and/or on the player's map. There are dialog branches that also allow the player to find out more about the world. But the game does not care at all whether the player explored all the additional dialog or not, and doesn't keep track of it, either. If the player asks the same question again, the NPC will give the same answer.

This type of dialog can have a "hub-and-spoke" chart:

The player meets the NPC at the "hub," where they can ask different questions. Each question leads the player into a narrative explanation of a topic. When they've exhausted that topic, they find themselves back at the hub. There they can nope out of the conversation, or pursue another one of the spokes.

As Alexander Freed wrote in *Game Developer*,[1]

> At their best, hubs make Players feel clever and in charge, picking and choosing how to approach their subjects in interrogation. At their worst, hubs turn NPCs into information vending machines where the Player feels obligated to punch every button and get each available tidbit of data. Such conversations lose any sort of naturalistic flow; pacing ceases to exist and voice acting becomes implausible as actors veer wildly from one subject to the next.

This format does allow some players to explore the game lore, while players who are just here to shoot aliens in the face can get to their face-shooting right away.

By comparison, in *Baldur's Gate 3*, dialog may contain information you might actually need to complete a quest. As a writer, this is so, so tempting. The player actually has to listen to the dialog! They can't just keep clicking buttons until the quest info appears in their journal! *BG3* goes further than that – there are books scattered here and there in the game world, and you need to read some of them in order to solve puzzles in the game! That's immersive, and it ties gameplay and narrative together!

That's much better than your typical Ubisoft "puzzle" where the solution is conveniently painted on the wall right next to the door, right?

However, this approach can be fraught. Some players will not understand even "obvious" clues. What is a simple verbal puzzle to the writer turns out to be impenetrable to them. They will then have to go read a walkthrough on the Internet, which makes some of that sweet, sweet immersion go away.

Consequently, most hub-and-spoke dialog is completely irrelevant to gameplay.

BRANCHING DIALOG FOR PLAYER EXPRESSION

Another reason to have branching dialog without branching story, though it's not that common, is for player expression. *Kentucky Route Zero* allows the player to choose different (text) responses to NPC dialog. It does not matter at all to the game which dialog option the player picks, but it hopefully means something to the player that they get to decide what sort of person their character is.

We prototyped something like this for *South of Midnight*. The player would be able to choose from three alternative lines, each of which would be in character for the protagonist. There would be an in-your-face line, a sarcastic line, and a straightforward line. The player gets to decide if their Hazel is sarcastic all the time, or confrontational, or not. This would have required a fair bunch of programming and would have tripled the amount of dialog we wrote and recorded, so we didn't do it.

CONVERSATIONAL CHALLENGES

It's possible to treat a branching conversation as a challenge that the player can succeed at or fail – just like a puzzle the player must solve or an enemy they must defeat. I haven't seen a lot of this sort of conversation.

Eidos-Montréal's *Deus Ex: Mankind Divided* (2011) and *Deus Ex: Human Revolution* (2013) have dialog challenges where Adam Jensen attempts to, for example, talk his way into the Detroit police station's morgue.

The player gets one chance to talk their way through it and has to live with the consequences. In the case of the police station in *Mankind Divided* (2011), if you fail to talk your way in, you have to fight your way in or sneak in through the vents.

The fun of this kind of challenge is that the player must really pay attention to the dialog to pick up the clues that enable them to "defeat" it. What makes Wayne Haas tick? What emotional buttons of his are there for you to push? The downside is that the conversation has to be written so that the clues *are* clear enough that the player can pick them up. I enjoyed the dialog challenges and felt they were fair, but some gamers on social media felt they could only guess randomly.

Rockstar's *LA Noire* (2011) was all about conversational combat – you have to try to talk your witnesses and suspects into revealing clues about the crimes you're investigating, and identify when they're lying. It was a great idea, but the system did not work spectacularly well; it seemed to ask the player to catch people lying based on how their faces were animated. The animation wasn't sophisticated enough to make that clear – and anyway, actual policemen can't tell whether people are lying based on their facial expressions. Human beings have been lying for two million years – we're good at it.

Big Bad Wolf's *The Council* (2018) also has conversations requiring you to be quick-witted. But the conversations are on a pretty short timer, making the conversational gameplay challenging indeed. If you don't pick a response, the game will pick for you, and you may not like how it picks. There's no good way around this short of saving and reloading often.

Dialog challenges in games are rare. They require a higher standard of writing than "keep pressing buttons for more info" style NPC quest-giving conversations. It's more challenging for the player, too, and some players will become frustrated by them. But there's something to be said for giving your players a reason to pay attention and use their own human experience in figuring out how to talk to a character.

A rule of thumb, though: unless the *point* of the game is conversational challenges, then a dialog challenge should only be difficult if there is an alternate path to the same goal. The player's experience shouldn't be ruined because they don't know what to say to people. Who wants to go back to high school?

PAY ATTENTION TO EMOTIONS

When you are giving the player multiple choices of what to say, the NPC's responses need to make logical *and emotional* sense no matter what they say.

I played a triple-A RPG once where I consistently chose the most obnoxious dialog lines for my character. Yet NPCs always responded politely and told me everything I needed to know to complete my next quest. The disconnect threw me right out of the game. When you're rude to people, they generally do not tell you how to get to the next step of your quest. They usually direct you to the nearest lake so you can go and jump in it.

Ideally, every line of player character dialog would have an NPC line that perfectly responded to it. However, that's a luxury few games have. You may need to make each of the main character's lines neutral enough that one NPC response works for all of them.

SOFTWARE

All these lines are a lot to keep in your head. If the dialog is linear, writers might use a screenwriting application like *Final Draft*, *Fade In*, or *Screenwriter* to write scenes. Barks are often written in a spreadsheet, which allows all sorts of neat sorting and formatting.

At some point, those scripts will be ported into an application that the audio department can use to keep track of lines as they are rendered into AI speech, temp voice recording, and final actor performances. In an indie company, that might be Microsoft Excel, Google Sheets, or another spreadsheet program.

Spreadsheets and screenwriting applications are not ideal for branching dialog. You don't want to have to write a Choose Your Own Adventure, "If player says this, go to paragraph 1173, but if player says that, go to paragraph 4019."

So, folks have made computer programs to track dialog branches. Applications like Twine (free) and Articy (cheap) allow you to write virtual index cards and draw arrows between them; they can then turn the index cards and arrows into HTML (web page), Unity, or Unreal Engine code to recreate that flow inside the computer.

Inkle, the company behind *80 Days*, *Overboard*, and *Pendragon*, among others, has its own free application for scripting branching dialog, called Ink, naturally.

AAA companies often have their own software that not only manages narrative flow but also makes it much easier to track dialog. For example,

Eidos-Montréal created a powerful dialog management application for *Guardians of the Galaxy* (2021).[2] Obsidian, developer of dialog-heavy open-world games like *Neverwinter Nights*, the *Fallout* series, and *Outer Worlds*, has its own bespoke software, too. I interviewed Narrative Director Lucian Soulban[3] when he worked there:

> It's a mind map, where it can expand outward into a variety of different responses. You can collapse responses or look at the tree in its entirety. You can highlight specific nodes through menu selection....
>
> It looks like a poster board with cards and branching lines on it. You'll put a card there: okay, this node is going to trigger three dialog options. And then you can add conditionals saying, well, this option is only triggered if the player has gone forward and finished the quest before ever talking to the NPC. If that condition isn't met, it then gives you just the other two options. Or this node is shared with multiple conversations. Coming from linear games, that's ... like going from chess to *Star Trek* 3D chess.

VOICES

How does dialog get into the game?

In days of old, we put the dialog on the screen as text. It was up to players to imagine how that character sounded. Many indie games, and for some reason the blockbuster *Zelda* games, still use this approach. It's cheap, fast, and simple.

However, there is nothing more expressive than the human voice. Great voice work propels a game to another level. That's why almost all AAA games are fully voiced with professional actors. And that's why, once *Disco Elysium* was a hit, the developers went back and recorded all the dialog they hadn't been able to afford on release.

Professionally recording voices is expensive. Recording studios and their highly skilled technicians charge a bunch of money. Professional actors charge high rates. They deserve those high rates. They have spent their lives training themselves to act, and they are lucky if they work one out of every three or four days in a year. If they didn't get paid exceptionally well for the days they do work, no one could afford to become a professional actor.

Temp Speech

Once a script is written, but before bringing actors in, developers will often use some sort of temporary placeholder recording.

Until a year or two ago, this was often "robo-speech": truly robotic-sounding text-to-speech. With the AI boom, artificial speech has improved from horrible to merely bad.

That's not entirely a good thing. The old robo-speech was *so* bad, other developers knew better than to use it to judge the quality of the writing. AI-driven artificial speech is close enough to human speech that devs sometimes forget it's not the real thing. What it doesn't sound like is human beings having emotional experiences, let alone actors having emotional reactions to imaginary circumstances.

AI can help you test that the dialog is in the right place. It can tell you if basic information is getting to the player, so they know where to go. It should *never* be used to evaluate dialog for narrative reasons. Clever lines will sound stupid in AI speech. Scenes will feel too long. You will have to keep reminding your fellow devs that it *is* fake speech.

Alternately, you can record yourself, your fellow developers, or anyone you can drag off the street and put in front of a microphone, to read your lines. Actual human beings are still vastly better at reading dialog than computers.

If you can scrape up even a small budget, consider hiring student actors from your local university, or local theater actors, rather than asking your fellow developers to voice characters.

Don't work too hard to clean up these temp voices. If they sound like they were recorded in a bedroom over Zoom, so much the better. You get the value of the human performance, but it's still clearly not the final product.

Casting

If you can get involved in the casting process without stepping on anyone's toes, do.

The key to getting great voice performances is spending too much time and effort on casting. The right actor will inhabit the role and nail the lines. The wrong actor may never give you the performance you need.

Because these are voice-acting gigs, actors don't have to come in physically for auditions. They will record your casting script (the "sides") at home, often in the almost professional-quality recording studio that they have rigged in a closet. They'll send their agent an MP3, though we still call these "self-tapes." Their agent will send it on to us.

For some roles, I've received 200 MP3s.

When going through self-tapes, I listen for four things:

- Do I believe the actor? Am I hearing someone read lines, or am I hearing a fictional character talking? Do *they* believe they are in the imaginary circumstances of the scene? This rules out as many as 80% of the self-tapes. Good actors inhabit the lines.
- Do they have an intention? Are they trying to get something they want? Sometimes an actor says a line more or less with the right intonation, but I don't have a sense that they want something.
- Who are they talking to? Are they talking to someone? You should have a sense of who they're saying the line *to.*
- Vocal charisma. Just like some actors have great presence on-camera – we call them "stars" – some actors' voices just "pop." They have distinctive voices that I want to hear more of. Others sound like everyone else.

You don't have to listen to the *whole* audition. If someone's wrong for the part, you often know it ten seconds in. Move on to the next.

When you get someone good, you'll know. You'll grin. You'll laugh out loud at your own lines. Ah-ha! Suddenly, you are not hearing an actor reading lines. *You are hearing the character speaking.*

Trust your innate bullshit detector. Human beings have really powerful ones. We know when something's not right. We can tell when the actor doesn't believe their own performance. This goes back to hunter-gatherer days. When your friend Og is telling you where to hunt deer or gather yummy roots, you need to know whether he is giving you a useful tip for feeding yourself and your beloved, or he is trying to feed you to a lion because he covets your beloved. Human beings who could tell the difference lived to have children.

Traditional vs. Method Acting

There are two main approaches to acting. The old tradition teaches controlling your voice and movements in a perfect simulacrum of a person having an emotional experience. The much more recent "Method" tradition teaches ways for the actor to actually have an emotional experience appropriate for an imaginary circumstance.

It is possible for really great actors in the old, British tradition to convince the audience that they are human beings in an imaginary circumstance.

But most of the time, while it can be entertaining, it is rarely convincing. It is just a lot easier to engage the audience emotionally if the actor is actually going through the emotion.

The audience may not know *why* they don't believe an actor; they may not even know *that* they don't believe the actor. But they will engage less with that actor's performance. Consequently, I have a strong preference for organic, Method-style acting.

Callbacks

To find the best actor for a role, you may go through literally hundreds of recorded auditions. You'll come out with a shortlist of a half dozen or so actors you want to call back for a second round. Callbacks also don't need to be in person. They can be over Zoom.

In a callback, I usually let the actor play the scene, then give them some adjustments. They do it again, and I give more adjustments. By the third take, they should be giving you what you're looking for, if they're capable of it.

Directing voice sessions is something senior (and some not-senior) video game writers often do, but how to direct is out of the scope of this book. Fortunately, there are zillions of books on how to direct actors. It can also be useful to take some acting classes, just to understand the acting process better. I took classes for two years at the Joanne Baron Studio in LA, and it helped my writing and directing more than three years of film school did.

There are few things more fun for a dramatic writer than watching their words go from letters on a page to being imaginatively lived by the right actor. The more knowledge you can bring to the process, the better the result will be.

I will leave you with one of the mysteries that poets and philosophers have struggled with in vain. If you give a good actor the script, and some description of the game and the role a week in advance, they will do a ton of homework, for free. Many AAA studios not only won't let their actors see the script before they show up in the studio for the recording session, they won't even tell the actors what character they're playing. The results speak for themselves.

NOTES

1 https://www.gamedeveloper.com/design/branching-conversation-systems-and-the-working-writer-part-2-design-considerations.
2 "Narrative Tools as Powerful as Marvel's 'Guardians of the Galaxy,'" GDC Narrative Summit 2022 talk by Rayna Anderson.
3 (Interview with author, https://complicationsensue.blogspot.com/2020/12/lucien-soulban-part-one.html).

CHAPTER 9

Rewriting

First, do no harm.

– *The Hippocratic Oath*

Any professional writer will tell you that writing is rewriting. Nobody's first drafts are perfect. Nor do they need to be, unless you are in so much of a crunch that you don't have time to rewrite. (Which can be fun, but that's another story.)

Video game development is iterative. You make something. You see how well it works. You fix or cut what doesn't work. You do more of whatever works. And then you do it again.

Once a movie has wrapped and post-production begins, it's a bear to go back and reshoot scenes. Often all you can do is fuss around the edges, cutting lines or scenes, and maybe re-recording some audio.

A video game is recreated by the engine from its data files every time it runs, so changing things is part of the process. Video game cutscenes get rewritten at the outline stage, at the draft stage, in the recording studio, in editing, and sometimes (rarely, it's expensive) after mo-cap and animation. A script or other narrative text is not done until you can't make it better – or it's time to take it to the recording studio – or your other priorities make it impossible to get back to it.

HOW TO TAKE CREATIVE CRITICISM

In this business, you'll get creative criticism from all sorts of people. Your boss, probably. Sometimes by co-workers. If you're smart, you'll ask for

DOI: 10.1201/9781003589068-9

criticism from people who report to you. Whenever the game comes out, you may get criticism from random strangers on the Internet, although that is rarely helpful.

Sometimes you will get notes that solve problems you are having. Some times you'll get notes you disagree with furiously.

None of us comes to creativity without an ego. To be a professional creative, by definition, is to want other people to have in their heads what you have in your head. If that's not important to you, you don't care. If you don't care, you won't do great work.

Ego regularly throws up obstacles to making creative criticism useful. How do you outwit your own ego?

Don't Take Criticism Personally

First of all, try not to take the feedback personally. This is hard to do. Someone is criticizing your baby! Obviously they hate you.

When you take criticism personally, it becomes an attack. If you're attacked, you defend yourself. If you defend yourself, you shut out the criticism.

Note that feedback, especially public feedback, sometimes *is* a personal attack. The bigger the company, the more likely it has politics. Sometimes people will indeed have it in for you. But you're still better off treating an attack as if it is sincere, constructive criticism, if only to judo your opponent into looking like a jerk.

All Sincere Feedback Is Legitimate

If someone says they don't like something, they don't like it. You can't tell yourself they *ought* to like it. If someone doesn't laugh at your joke, it's not funny, at least to them. If someone says they're confused, then your writing confused them. If someone says they hate a character, then they hate them. It's on you to figure out why, and what to do about it.

Jon Ingold again: "All feedback is an emotional reaction to something, and you have to unpick what that something was before you can deal with it."[1]

You may be getting criticism from someone who does not even like the genre you're working in. What you choose to do with that information – whether you feel it is not relevant, or you embrace it – is up to you. But their criticism (if sincere) is still *valid* in the sense that that is their experience.

Distance Yourself

It helps not to think of the work as your baby. Think of it as "the" baby. Don't call it "my" scene, it's "the current draft of the scene." This also gives other people permission to critique it more freely. You can even criticize the work yourself. Maybe you have an idea of something that's wrong with it, that you haven't had time to fix, or don't know how to fix.

Critiquing your own work, incidentally, makes anything positive that you might say about it more believable.

The Problem May Not Be Where They Think It Is

Just because all feedback is legitimate doesn't mean that your note-giver is right about what the problem is. They may be picking at a symptom, not the cause.

Neil Gaiman: "When people tell you something's wrong or doesn't work for them, they are almost always right. When they tell you exactly what they think is wrong and how to fix it, they are almost always wrong."

I studied computer science at university. In programming, if something goes wrong three quarters of the way through, it's often because you didn't set something up properly at the beginning. In the narrative, someone will say a scene is too long. But shortening the scene will not make the scene better. That's because the real problem is earlier, where the game story failed to make you care about the characters.[2]

Jon Ingold: "'I found the story slow' is often code for 'I didn't like the main character.'"[3]

Bear in mind, if you show someone a scene, they won't have in their head all the scenes that went before it. You'll know who the characters are, but they may not. It's up to you to interpret the feedback you get.

Assume They Are Not an Idiot

However, before you go off and decide that they're wrong about the problem, allow for the possibility that the person giving you a note is not an idiot. There are almost no *stupid* people in video games.

What often happens is, when someone gives a suggestion, what pops into our mind is an idiotic version of it. You think they want a sweeping change. You feel like they're trying to cut the heart out of the scene. Why would they want *that*? That's just *dumb*!

Before you reject their identification of a problem, try to figure out what a *non*-idiotic version of what they're saying might be. "If this *wasn't* dumb, what would it be?" Then ask if the non-idiotic version is what they meant. If it is, bravo! Now you have a good problem to solve instead of a bad one. But even if they did mean something dumb, at least they are clearer on what you're thinking, and you're clearer on what they're thinking; and you have identified a non-idiotic problem your work might have.

Sometimes you will get a criticism that seems unconvincing or totally beside the point or just generally "whaaaaa?" Someone will say, "But she could never wear a hat because she has pointy ears."

It is usually futile to point out that, say, the hat could have holes for the ears, because the unconvincing comment is not the real objection. The real objection is something stronger, but they are having trouble unpacking it and they don't know how to explain it. So they pick at something else more concrete. You need to have a conversation to pull out of them what their real problem is.

Find the Truth

Back in the previous millennium, my acting teacher used to say, "Find the truth." It's easy to find something in feedback that might give you an excuse to dismiss all of it. "They are definitely wrong about x, so they are probably also wrong about y, z, a, b and c." You will often get more benefit from figuring out in what way is this true or what part of this is true than in figuring out why it's wrong.

Search for what is true rather than what is false. Figure out *how* the critique is true. Or, what is this true *of*?

Your goal isn't to defend your work. Your goal is to find how it is weak. Actively seek out the criticism, even if it is buried in confusion, contradiction, or fluff.

Try running with the criticism instead of shooting it down. The key phrase in improv is "yes, and." If the actor you're with says "I'm a pineapple," then you can't say, "No, you're not." That would kill the improv. You can say, "And I'm a grocer" or "and I'm an orange" or "and I'm a pineapple fetishist."

The hard part of science is not finding evidence that corroborates your theory. The hard part is thinking up ways to *disprove* your theory. If you try to disprove your theory every which way, and it holds up, it's a solid theory. But if you only try to support it, you're leaving it to other people to point out its flaws.

Actively *dig for* the truth. Sometimes people will point out something that, you agree, is a problem. But you also get the feeling that something else is bugging them. They just can't crystallize what it is. So they grumble at it and move on.

This is often a much more structural, serious problem than the thing they were able to criticize. It will require more work to fix. The temptation is to avoid the hint and focus on the surface flaw.

Don't ignore it. Interrogate them (nicely). Try to work with them to crystallize what they're having problems with. When someone tells you, "Nah, forget it, it's fine," you say, "No, seriously. I can tell you're bumping on something. Let's talk about it."

If you don't, they will come back with the same criticism in three months. Or, play-testers will have the same problem. Or, God forbid, players.

Don't wait for the snippy Let's Play video. Dig.

What They Want You to Do about It May Be Wrong

All feedback is legitimate. Most criticisms have some truth to them.

Many solutions proposed to you will be bad. Hopefully, a more experienced writer can give you an approach that will solve the problem. Other people, particularly non-writing managers and people from other disciplines, will give you suggestions that fix the problem in front of you and create many more problems elsewhere. Even your boss may give you a bad idea, if you spent a month thinking through what you wrote, and they're skimming it during an online conference call about optimizing frame rates.

Feel free to take the good bits of the criticism and ignore the bad solutions. Unless, of course, where you are, congeniality is prized over creative results. (That's called "toxic positivity," and most senior developers have experienced it one time or another.)

Find Out What Problem They Are Trying to Solve

Surprisingly often, people forget to give you their critique or gloss over it. They jump right to their solution.

It's wise to find out what they're trying to fix before addressing – or rejecting – their solution. They may be proposing a big, involved solution to a problem you can fix surgically, in a line or two.

Or, you may realize that the problem they brought up is actually bigger than their solution, and is going to require more work. That's useful to know, too, even if it is not cheery news.

"We'll Take a Look at That."

So, you really worked at understanding the criticism, and you know what their problem really is. But you're still convinced that they're wrong. They're honing in on something that's not the real problem, they want something fixed that isn't broken, they want a change that will break things, they didn't game it out.

You may find yourself from time to time in a situation where you can already see their idea won't work. You can work it out in your head. Or maybe you already tried it out, like, three months ago. It didn't work then, and it's not gonna work now.

Imagining how unwritten things are going to turn out, whether they're going to play nice together, what they're going to break – this is a writer's superpower. Surprisingly, most non-writers cannot do the math in their heads. They can't *imagine* doing the math in their heads. So when you tell them you already did it, and that's not going to work, they won't believe you. They'll think you are being precious. They may feel disrespected.

I got in hot water for telling folks about problems I could foresee in a story. Two years later, sure enough, the story still had those problems. (Didn't help me any, but I was already at another company.)

Say, "We'll take a look at that."

Then really do take a look at it. Actually. Really truly.

That gives you time to remember that the person who gave you the note is probably not an idiot, to find the truth, to find the deeper problem, etc. Time for your hackles to come down. Time to try out the suggestion, so you can say, "I tried it, and I couldn't make it work." Or "that doesn't work but how about this?" Or "it works if we do it *this* way."

Or, "I tried your idea and it worked. Thank you!" That generally goes down pretty well.

(You can even say this when they didn't propose anything, but their notes triggered a good idea on your part. Or when they proposed something only tangential to what you did. They will often agree that it was their idea.

When I was a kid, we were told that we should be truthful about everything. But we were also told that avocado was a good color for a kitchen, so we should have known better.)

Sometimes They Just Want to Be Heard

Sometimes you don't have to make any changes at all to your work. Sometimes it's enough to simply nail down exactly what the other person's concern is, and what they want you to do about it. Sometimes people just want to know you take them seriously. A narrative director I've worked with had to deal with a programmer who was full of bad ideas. He took the guy out to lunch every two weeks and listened to all his ideas. The guy was very happy when the game went out, because of all the input he'd had, even though none of it was implemented. Go figure.

Needless to say, do not *assume* this is the case. Just be aware of it as a possibility.

Is It a Hill to Die on?

Sometimes you have to execute a note you think is wrong. Videogames are a collaborative art. If you don't execute the note the way higher-ups want, at some point they will find someone who will.

Play the long game. If you were right, at some point it may become clear that the note did not work. If there's time and resources, perhaps it will get fixed. And, you know, maybe you were wrong. There have been times I thought I was right, and I was wrong, you know?

Kim MacAskill told me,

> There are so many moving pieces at a time, it's kind of choosing your battles. Sometimes, okay, that's going to wreck that scene, and that's going to wreck the story, and you sit down with yourself and go, Okay, is this when I fight the battle? Is this the day when I push back?
>
> It can be hard, because when you're so invested in your story, you have to ask, have they actually killed the story dead, or is it recoverable, or can I even make it better?
>
> It's a constant compromise. Really living and breathing your characters and caring about them and then someone telling you that you can't tell the story that you intended. But am I really annoyed, or am I just tired? It's a constant self-mental-assessment.[4]

Ask yourself, is this a hill to die on?

Honestly, it probably isn't. Probably.

I mean, if someone asks you to write something legit evil, then yeah, kick up a fuss.

But if they're just asking you to write something dumb, well, it's a video game. Video games are sometimes dumb. Your career is more important than a video game.

Your job, really, is not to make a good game. Your job is to make your team happy. If you can do that by making a good game, God bless us one and all. But if your team is unhappy, they're just going to fix what they think you broke, and you won't have done the game any favors. But if you make them happy, you might learn something.

FORESTALLING CRITICISM

"It is easier to get forgiveness than permission." In most cases, the wisest course is to tell your colleagues what you want to do before you do it. If you ask their advice and then follow it, it's much harder for them to criticize than if you present a *fait accompli* they had no part in.

However, in a few cases, you may have an idea you think will work great, but which you suspect will engender a huge discussion in which your idea gets lost. In those rare cases, you may want to just forge ahead and do the thing. If it works seamlessly, people may not even realize you've done it. For one game, I wanted to give a jazzy name to a key event in lore. If I'd asked what we wanted to call it, I might have got stuck with something I didn't like. Instead, I simply started calling it by a new name, and it caught on.

For another game, I had an idea about the very end of the game. I knew that the creative director wasn't on board with it, but I just kept pitching it to people, and it caught on. Once he started hearing it from all directions, he got on board.

You don't want to do that more than once or twice a game, though. Once or twice, you may get the benefit of the doubt. If it becomes a habit, then you're just going rogue, and that's a bad reputation to have.

HOW TO GIVE CREATIVE CRITICISM

Giving criticism well is as hard as taking criticism well. In taking criticism well, your goal is not to get your back up. In giving it well, your goal is not to get the other person's back up.

Assume They Will Take Your Notes Personally

Remember how I suggested that you not take notes personally? Assume that other people will.

Everyone knows you're not supposed to have your ego wrapped up in your work. You're supposed to be objective, willing to cut, and willing to change. But no one comes to creativity without an ego.

That doesn't mean don't give criticism. I'm just saying, don't count on people being happy about getting it.

Don't trust people! People will sometimes ask for critiques and then get mad when you give them one.

Who knows? Maybe they really di honestly want notes, until you gave them your notes.

How can you tell if someone really wants notes? The way they react. Start with compliments. Or a small note. If they say, "Fine, fine, sure, thanks, but seriously, tell me what you're bumping on," they're legit. Basically, if they behave like I suggest you behave when you're getting notes.

If they say, "Tell me the worst ha ha that is practically a giveaway that what they really want is compliments.

As the poet Maya Angelou said, "People will forget what you said. People will forget what you did. But people will never forget how you made them feel."

The Sandwich

Criticisms goes down less painfully when they are sandwiched between slices of praise. People judge experiences first by how they feel at the end, and then how they felt at the beginning.

Cognitive psychology confirms this. Ask someone to put their hand in ice water for 20 seconds, and rate their discomfort. Then ask them to put their hand in ice water for 20 seconds, followed by 10 seconds in chilly water. They will rate the second, longer exposure as *less* unpleasant, not more. Humans are stupid that way.

What if you just don't like the work? You're probably not trying hard enough to find something nice to say about it.

But even if you don't like anything about it, make something up. You're creating making up a whole world surely you can make up a compliment?

I once told a writer something was good, and he said, "oh, you hate it." I said, "no, if I'd hated it, I would have said it was a good start.

Clarify What Kind of Information They Are Looking for

So *how* do you give negative notes with as little pain as possible? Start by clarifying in what stage they consider the work to be.

Is this a rough draft and they're willing to rethink the whole idea? Do they want to hear about structural problems?

Or, are they pretty sure their structure is fine, and they just want to know if the characters sound right?

Or, do they honestly just want a cookie?

When I have given notes badly, I have sometimes given notes that are, in principle, brilliant. I might notice a structural flaw in a dialog scene. Say the characters don't really want anything from each other. No drama.

There is a time for that note. And there is a point after which it's not helpful. If a scene or level or asset has been approved by a slew of higher-ups, or God forbid, made by them, then the person you're giving notes to may not feel safe rethinking it. In that case, you will make a friend by suggesting how to paint it another color or put a nice hat on it – anything to take the curse off of it.

It's not what's best for the game, overall. But it may be what's best *now*. There is no point in giving a note that cannot be implemented, and you won't make a friend doing it.

What Were They Trying to Do?

It may be useful to ask what they were trying to accomplish. What is this asset for? If something does not appear to be working, could it be because you don't understand what it's supposed to be doing? Once you do understand what it's supposed to be doing, you might be able to suggest a simpler or stronger way of doing it.

Unless the thing you are criticizing is inherently contrary to the vision or voice of the game, try to critique it on its own terms. The spirit of it should be "I think what you are trying to do is X, and you can make it more X if you do this." Not, "Here's how I would have done it."

Clarify What Is the Thing They Most Love

Clarify what is most dear to the heart of the person whose work you are criticizing. It is not rare that the thing they are proudest of is the problem. When someone is fond of a bit of work, they tend to protect it at the expense of the whole.

As Arthur Quiller-Couch said in 1914:

> Whenever you feel an impulse to perpetrate a piece of exceptionally fine writing, obey it—whole-heartedly—and delete it before sending your manuscript to press. Murder your darlings.

But you have to be delicate when you suggest to someone that they kill their darlings. You should gently acknowledge how terribly fine their darling is. Explain how it is both good and also wrong. If possible, suggest some other place it might work better.

Clarify Your Purpose in Giving Notes

Examine your own heart. Why are you giving this particular note? It's not to show how smart you are, is it? Those notes are best kept to yourself. Make sure your motives are pure.

You don't have to give every note. The classic advice for a woman dressing up is: after you're happy with how you look, remove one thing.

A great tennis coach doesn't try to fix your grip, your swing, your stance, and your spin all at once.

Which are the notes that may get resolved without you saying anything? You don't have to give those.

Which notes will someone else probably give if you don't? You don't have to give those, either.

Which notes call out the symptoms of the problem, and which call out the causes? If you can fix the causes, you don't have to mention the symptoms.

Nobody likes getting a whole flock of notes, which is reason I try not to give a flock. But also, if you give too many notes, your colleague may just do the easy fixes and ignore the most important fixes.

Try to Avoid Giving Harsh Notes in Public

Ideally possible, avoid giving big bad notes in public. Adding witnesses adds stress. If the person you're giving notes to feels embarrassed, they will reject your notes, and possibly try to get back at you. Trust me on this one.

You may be asked to give your notes in a meeting. You may want to suggest not doing that. Remember how I said people can't be trusted?

There are exceptions. If the notes might be valuable to other listeners – for example, in a class – then there's a point to giving them publicly. But make sure to stick to general principles.

Try to Avoid Giving Harsh Notes in Writing

Also, try to avoid giving harsh notes in a document or in chat. Do it "live" if possible. Then you can gauge how they're going over, and if they don't go over well, you can trim them down, or if they are going down very badly indeed, discover a personal emergency that you have to attend to immediately. It is also better to involve the note-receiver in a discussion so that they feel more ownership of the notes.

You may need to give notes in writing, if you are in a different time zone, or you are communicating with someone whose first language is not yours. I have given written notes to my Chinese colleagues in Hangzhou, because they can absorb them at their own speed -- and we have software to translate written notes instantaneously.

If you must give notes only on paper, then be very, very careful to make sure they are phrased very gently, and there's nothing in them that can be misinterpreted or misquoted.

How to Phrase Notes

You can phrase your notes to diminish how hurtful they feel. For example,

Convey personal feelings, not absolute observations.

Absolute statements are dangerous. If you say something is a certain way, where do you get off saying that? Are you God?

Much less dangerous are personal statements. When you talk about your own reaction, you are on solid ground. If you say you had a reaction, who can say you didn't?

For example, compare these two notes:

- Boy, that character design is creepy.
- Boy, that character design gives me the creeps.

These two sentences carry the same meaning. When you say something *is* creepy, you're really saying that you get a creepy feeling from it. But saying it *is* creepy comes across as an objective judgment. Which it is not. So, make clear that this is just your personal feeling. The recipient will, in any event, decide whether or not your personal feeling matters. But they are less likely to be offended by your personal feeling than by your objective judgment.

- This level isn't scary.
- This level didn't scare me.

The recipient may feel threatened by the first statement (assuming we are talking about a horror game). They are less likely to feel threatened by the second.

- That dialog is garbled.
- I couldn't understand what the NPC is saying.

Your reaction may be universal. It may also turn out to be idiosyncratic. Maybe you had trouble understanding the dialog when other players will understand it just fine. You're giving the same information to the recipient, which is that you found the dialog to be garbled. But you are not a user research team. You are just one person. So speak only for yourself.

If you are a user research team, of course, then you can be much more specific: "four out of ten players were unable to answer these three questions after listening to the dialogue." In that case, of course, your recipient shouldn't feel personally attacked because you are conveying other people's opinions, not your own. Hey, you thought it was great.

Make Positive Statements, Not Negative Ones.

Any negative statement can be a positive. American traffic signs say, "no left turn!" with a big left-turn arrow underneath an alarming red "no, don't!" circle. In Quebec, traffic signs say, "you can go straight or turn left," with arrows pointing ahead and to the right, in a comforting green "go ahead!" circle.

- I have no idea what I'm supposed to do here.
- Let's make it clearer what the player is supposed to do here.

There is not a lot of difference between the *meaning* of the negative and positive versions. But the negative one says, "your material sucks." The positive ones say, "Your material could be better."

Well, of course, it could be better. Anything can be better. Saying that doesn't hurt as much.

- That looks muddy.
- The colors could be brighter.

No one wants to hear that their colors are muddy. But, okay, maybe they could be brighter.

- This cinematic goes on too long.
- This cinematic could be shorter.

No one likes to hear bad things about their baby. However, they are sometimes willing to hear how their baby could be better.

Underexaggerate.

Phrase things so they are unarguable. You don't want people picking at whether your statement is literally true. So, phrase things so they are practically impossible to dispute. You would think that would weaken what you're saying. Weirdly, it doesn't.

- We are so fucked.
- Our situation is … non-optimal.

Said in the right tone of voice, a very mild statement can convey the sense of a radical statement.

I learned this one dealing with a particular teenager. I learned not to say, "you lie all the time" and instead to say "y'know, you don't always tell the truth."

- It's a cliché.
- It's not the first time we've seen it.

It's easy for the recipient to disagree that something is a cliché. But it's hard to disagree that we've seen it before at least once. The recipient will nonetheless know that they need to look at whether the thing is a cliché or not.

- This level is impossible.
- So, this is harder than Animal Crossing.

Southerners will sometimes say things like, "Well, that's better than a poke in the eye with a sharp stick." Most things are better than a poke in the eye with a sharp stick. But it becomes an amusing, and indisputable, way of conveying that something is good indeed.

Questions instead of statements

- I have no idea what I'm supposed to do here.
- What do I do here?
- We have nothing to root for here.
- What are we rooting for here?

"I have no idea what I'm supposed to do here" and "We have nothing to root for here" may both come across as attacks. You're making the note-getting feel stupid and inept.

"What do I do here?" isn't an attack; it's a request for help. And it's easy for the note-getting to answer. They can just tell you what you're supposed to do there. They will still, nonetheless, get the implicit criticism. If you had to ask what you should do, that needs to be clearer. If you are asking what to root for, then that needs to be clearer, too.

I Thought I Was Dealing with Professionals

Do professionals really need all this handling and ego stroking?

Not always. Once you've been working with someone long enough, you may feel confident that they just want honest criticism. I've worked with writers who felt comfortable telling me, "Here's why I hate that," and I thought that was great.

But it's a good idea to phrase critiques carefully, as questions, as personal observations, as positive statements. There is very little downside to doing it. You can communicate exactly the same ideas; they just go down smoother.

Should You Offer a Solution?

This is tricky. When you see a flaw in something, you will often think of a way to fix it.

However, the moment you offer a solution, then the discussion is no longer about whether your critique is right or not; it becomes about whether your solution is good.

On the other hand, there is a danger that if you don't offer a solution, it may feel like you are just insulting the work. I have been dinged for both!

How do you square this circle?

In some cases, you may want to lead with, "I have a note, but it's something that can be fixed."

You may want to bury the lede. Wait for the other person to absorb the critique. Then say, "I had an idea how to solve this surgically."

And it *can* be fixed. With enough time and money, anything can be fixed.

Either way, let them ask for your solution before you give it.

Listening Is Not the Same as Agreeing

People will often fail to address your notes. That does not mean they are ignoring you. They may be listening to you; they just don't agree with your analysis. They may not have understood your notes; that's on you. They may have found that some issue you didn't see is blocking them from addressing your note.

They may also be ignoring you, of course.

When Can You Give Notes without All These Shenanigans?

There is one time it might be a good idea to blithely give it to them straight. Suppose people are considering hiring you to fix something. Suppose you don't want the job unless you can do a good job. Then you can tell them straight out what's wrong and how you want to fix it – provided you're willing to walk away if they don't like what you say.

If they hire you anyway, you have a mandate to fix the things you don't like. If they don't hire you, you're off the hook. You won't have to work on something you're not allowed to fix.

A WORD ABOUT "OWNERSHIP"

There is an idea that writers should "own" some section of the game, or one or more narrative delivery systems. That means that they have primary responsibility over the narrative elements. A writer might own Level 5 or all environmental narratives.

Primary responsibility does not mean final authority. A writer should expect to be rewritten by more experienced writers – or, sometimes, the creative director, or the voice director, or God forbid, the actor or a producer. It's good not to get precious about your writing. You got the fun of writing it. And you got paid for it. (That's why they call it "compensation.") The game's needs trump any one person's desire to leave a mark on it.

Ownership can get in the way of the production's needs. It may be that Level 5 has to be completely rewritten. It might be that the whole team needs to jump on Level 5 and fix it; you can't allow the production to slow down because the writer who owns the level can't get it all done at once.

LISTEN TO THE GAME

In the beginning, the team is trying to achieve their vision for the game.

At a certain point in development or production, their original vision becomes almost irrelevant. The game has taken shape. There is something the game *wants* to be, and that is almost never the game you wanted to make, not exactly. You are wise to help it become what it wants to become.

The same thing may be true of the story you are telling. You planned to tell one story, but now the game is telling a different story. You need to tell *that* story as well as you can, unless you can neatly trim your old story to fit the new structure.

Listen to the game. Hopefully, the new thing that the game wants to be is better than what you originally planned. But you will force it back to the old vision only at the cost of carnage. Money and time, certainly. Sometimes morale. And the game may never be as good as what it was organically trying to be.

We started *We Happy Few* trying to make a roguelike. We put a lot of effort into the procedural generation of the map. But when we took the game to show at Pax East, early on, players told us that what they liked was the little bespoke scenarios we had crafted and put into the map. The game wanted to be less about random encounters and more about strange ones.

So we made a game with tons of strange encounters. We were stuck with the procedural generation for the main game, but we dropped it for the DLCs.

That's not to say that a game can't get horribly off track. The game needs to end up with one single vision. If the game is trying to be three things at once, that will not do. Pick one and make that game.

The craft of rewriting is figuring out what the best things that you have are, and how to make those things stronger. The greatest editors – Ezra

Pound editing T. S. Eliot, Brian Eno producing David Bowie – simply help the artist take the work in the direction it wants to go.

Hopefully, you figure that out while there's still time. One of the familiar tragedies of game development is that every game *eventually* teaches you how you should have made it, and what you should have made it into. I have an opinion about what we shoulda done on *South of Midnight* – but I didn't figure it out until long after we were committed to another approach.

PLAY OTHER GAMES…

While you're listening to the game, listen to other games. You should be playing lots of narrative games, particularly games like the one you're working on.

Of course, you are playing games for fun. I assume you're here because you love games! I mean, there are easier ways of making money. And you need to be able to talk intelligently about gameplay and narrative mechanics with other devs.

You also need to be playing games for research. That means playing at least a little most of the games that everyone's talking about at the office, on your Discords, on your Bluesky feed, or on the hellsite. Those may not be narrative games. Everyone on my social media fell in love with *Balatro*. At one point, they were all talking about *Blaseball*.

Non-writing devs sometimes have a suspicion that the writers, especially women writers, aren't serious about playing games and would really rather be cuddled up with a novel. That's ridiculous, of course, but it's good to inoculate yourself against it by regularly mentioning games you've played.

One of the nice things about the video game industry is you can show up to work late, saying, "Sorry, I track of the time playing this game, and suddenly it was light outside," and people's response will be "whoa, righteous!" Or, "I need to take off Thursday, because *Baldur's Gate 3* is coming out."

But you are not just playing games for street cred. You are playing games to experience them as a player. A lot of times when I'm responding to an idea, and it's out of my immediate expertise as a narrative guy, I'll say, "As a player, this would make me feel X." (Sometimes I also say "as a player" when I feel that folks are not taking my expertise as a narrative guy seriously enough. It happens.)

And, of course, you are playing them to understand the narrative mechanics. The narrative exists to give players the feels. So you need to play narrative games two ways. The first time, or the first few hours, to see how you feel. The second time, or later on in the game, to figure out, "How does this game make me feel that?" and "Is this game succeeding in what it want to make me feel?" and "Is there a better way it could be making me feel that?"

As a side benefit, you can play games at home and explain to your partner or your mom that you are, in fact, working, because you are.

... BUT CONSUME OTHER MEDIA!

Of course, don't just play games this way. Watch movies and TV and read books this way. What did it make me feel? How did it make you feel that? Not every technique in films or books translates to a game, but the pillars of storytelling are the same in all human media.

As an exercise: what would be a gameplay mechanic that would help the player feel that if the movie/TV show/book were a game?

You cannot travel as many places in the world as you can in books; some of the best don't even exist. You cannot meet all the most interesting people in the real world; you can meet many more in fiction.

Feed your head, as the Dormouse said. You need to put things into your head in order to be able to take things out. And you need a sense of what stories have been told before, and how, so you can keep your work fresh.

HOW TO USE AI

We've all been hearing a lot about the use of generative artificial intelligence – large language models or LLMs – in writing. Some executives think they can get rid of a lot of writers by using AI. For example, barks. Couldn't ChatGPT come up with a lot of barks? And quests? And stories? And backstories?

Fortunately for me, generative artificial intelligence is not intelligent. Large language models literally do not know what they're talking about. Generative AI takes a prompt and then searches through an enormous database to figure out what text is most likely to show up after this prompt. Not the smartest or the best answers, just the most likely one. Generative AI is Big Autocomplete.

That means if you ask a generative AI a question, you are getting the average answer based on its training data. If you ask it to write something for you, you'll get a rehash of what everyone else has already done.

Good writing comes out of your distinctiveness. Your personality. Your experience of life. It is filtered through who you are. It has your voice. We are not hiring you to give us the same old same old. We are hiring you to come up with something surprising. Something heartfelt. Something that gets a rise out of you and therefore might get a rise out of the reader, the audience, or the player.

If you ask generative AI for barks, it will give you the least surprising barks ever. The most average. The most boring.

If you ask it for stories, it will give you stories you've heard before, unless it gives you stories that make no sense at all.

So, how can you use large language models in your writing?

Simple: it can tell you what to avoid.

Ask it to give you barks. DO NOT USE THE ONES IT SHOWS YOU. Make up other ones.

Ask it to give you plots. DO NOT USE ITS PLOTS. THEY ARE TIRED.

Working with LLMs can teach you to take your writing beyond the expected. It will give you the expected. If you write away from or around what's expected, your writing will become unexpected. Fresh. Original.

Or you can take its plots and then twist them – which is what pro writers do all the time. We're not making up plots from scratch all the time; 90% of the time, what we write is like something else, but twisted, subverted, or redoubled in some way. (This appropriation and adaptation of earlier, better writer's work is called "culture.")

Use gen AI as a warning. If gen AI came up with something, it's too tired for you to use.

NOTES

1 Interview with author, October 14, 2020. https://complicationsensue.blogspot.com/2020/10/jon-ingold-part-two.html.

2 As this book was going to press, Neil Gaiman was accused of rape by multiple women https://www.vulture.com/article/neil-gaiman-allegations-controversy-amanda-palmer-sandman-madoc.html.

3 Interview with author, October 14, 2020. https://complicationsensue.blogspot.com/2020/10/jon-ingold-part-two.html.

4 Interview with author on author's blog, *Complications Ensue*, August 26, 2020.

CHAPTER 10

Breaking into Video Game Writing

GETTING YOUR FIRST JOB

I am not an expert in getting a first game writing job. I have only done it once. Strangely, this is also true of my friends. None of them has ever gotten more than one first job.

How I did it was: I was a professional film and television writer. I was one of the writers on a movie called *Bon Cop/Bad Cop*, a bilingual French/English buddy cop comedy about hockey murders strongly "inspired" by *Lethal Weapon*. It was a massive hit in Québec; it broke the Canadian box office record for a local movie.

I organized a panel discussion at McGill University in which four video game writers explained their jobs to a hundred or so screenwriters. I moderated the panel. I organized it with the help of Jason Della Rocca, then head of the Montreal chapter of the International Game Developers' Association.

So, when Compulsion Games was looking for a writer for *Contrast*, they asked Jason who they should talk to. He suggested me. They thought, holy smoke, *Bon Cop/Bad Cop*? They met me, they liked me. So, they hired me.

I pontificated my way in.

So, *one* way into game writing is to be a successful writer in an adjacent field and know someone who will give you a call when some folks need a writer.

DOI: 10.1201/9781003589068-10

There is not one well-established, surefire way to break into the game business as a writer. Here are a few things you need:

1. Access.
2. Portfolio.
3. Resume aka CV.
4. Knowledge of games.
5. A personable cover letter.

ACCESS

You need to know where the jobs are and have a way to reach the companies that have them.

Access is, in principle, not that hard. Many game writing jobs are posted on LinkedIn. They may also be posted on GamesIndustry.biz, Grackle HQ, MobyGames, WorkWithIndies.com, Hitmarker, and other job aggregating sites. The big studios have their own sites with job listings.

You might also hear of jobs through social media. Some accounts aggregate game jobs. There are Discord servers, such as the Discord for Interactive Narrative, that have channels devoted to game jobs. There are grassroots organizations that help diverse writers; Pixelles, for example, helps women and non-binary writers.

There is a lot of competition for those jobs, because everyone else has a computer and a modem, or a phone, too. It's better to know about jobs before they're advertised. You want to have an inside track.

If you are working at a company in a non-writing job, that's an inside track. Larger companies have internal job boards, where they post jobs before they're public. And if your fellow devs know you're looking to write, and they like you, they'll let you know about jobs before they're posted.

A lot of people I know got their first game job in Quality Assurance, that is, playtesting. I know an artist who became a narrative designer. Any job that gets you in the door and teaches you how games get made can be helpful.

WRITE!

Find the people responsible for narrative at your company and ask them if you can do some writing, on top of your other responsibilities. I can't speak for other folks, but I have never turned down someone in my company asking me for a shot to prove they can write. There's always something that could be written that no one has time to write.

The key is to not be picky. If it was a super fun writing assignment, someone would already have grabbed it. The task may be "update the game bible." That's not glorious work and it's not even player-facing, but it's still an opportunity to show that you can write, that you're fun to work with, and that you turn things in on time. As one author says about freelance work,

> You get work however you get work, but people keep working because their work is good, because they are easy to get along with and because they deliver the work on time. And you don't even need all three! Two out of three is fine. People will tolerate how unpleasant you are, if your work is good and you deliver it on time. People will forgive the lateness of your work, if it is good and they like you. And you don't have to be as good as everyone else if you're on time and it's always a pleasure to hear from you.[1]

If someone asks you to write something, anything, for a game, then jump at the chance. If no one asks, offer.

My wife, Lisa, long ago, worked at *Natural History* magazine, in a job where she was not paid to write things. She found a book and suggested they review it. They didn't feel like reviewing it, so they asked if she wanted to review it herself. She pulled an all-nighter and wrote a great book review. After that, they went to her for more book reviews. Now, she gets paid to write things.

When I was in film school, I was offered a lousy $1,000 to write a draft ($600) and two rewrites ($200 each) of a cheesy exploitation action movie. I jumped on it. They stiffed me out of the last $200! (You're not a real professional screenwriter until they've stiffed you out of at least $50,000.) But I'm not sad I wrote it. You have to get all the bad screenplays out before the good ones come.

I'm amazed how many self-proclaimed writers don't jump at every chance they get to write. Folks in my company have asked me to help them get into writing. I've thrown them work to do, and they didn't do it. Don't be precious. All those kung fu movies where the hero has to start by sweeping the dojo? If no one is asking you to sweep, you're ahead of the game.

You can also meet people at various industry get-togethers. There may be an IGDA (International Game Developer's Association) chapter in your area. There may be other game industry meetups. I worked with someone who got her first job from a creative director with whom she struck up a friendship at a meetup.

When you know someone well enough, ask if you can buy them a cup of coffee. When I was coming up, almost everyone was willing to have a coffee with me. And I've had coffee with a lot of people coming up. But you generally only get one coffee. After the first, you need to be bringing something of value to the other person.

It's easier to meet someone if you're asking for advice than if you're asking for a job. As the proverb goes, "Ask for advice, get a job. Ask for a job, get advice."

PORTFOLIO

Access gets you in the door. After that, you have to show that you can deliver the goods.

It's important to have a portfolio. You're trying to show that you can write inventively but you can also write to order. You have your own voice, but you can write in the voice of the game. You can write a variety of narrative delivery systems and knock it out of the park in each.

Your portfolio could include some of:

- A dramatic cutscene of three to five pages between two characters with distinct voices, each trying to get something from the other and using their words to try to get it. Surprisingly few game writers have this. Note that this is *not* an exposition scene where someone tells someone else some lore or gives a quest. It's dramatic.

- A sample of barks. What are 10 or 15 ways to say, "I need healing!" I have seen portfolios where the writer gives me two lines for 15 different situations. That proves nothing. Anyone can write two lines for a situation. It only starts to be a challenge after the first five or six lines. After ten, it really starts to be difficult to convey what the bark is supposed to convey, differently than in the first ten, in a very short line, without sounding weird. ("Forsooth! A grenade!")

- Many portfolios include lore pages. Faux histories of an imaginary fantasy world are less impressive than, say, short, juicy descriptions of game items such as guns, swords, or potions.
- A branching story or branching dialog. You can write something in Twine, Ink, or Articy, and turn it into a playable game, so people can play it on the Internet. Make sure it is surprising, witty, and moving. For example, Matthew Burns and Tom Bissell's hilarious and heartbreaking *The Writer Will Do Something* (2015) which is available on Itch.io. I hired one writer largely on the basis of an interactive novel they wrote and programmed. It showed they could create a feeling using words. Aleah Churchill's site (http://leahchurchill.com) has a five-minute game also hosted on Itch.io where an asteroid is about to wipe out the Earth in five minutes, and your ex mysteriously texts you, "Hey…." It shows she can create characters and voices and can bring the funny.
- A mod. Many games allow you to create entire quests using the game's assets and engine. In the past, I've seen writing tests along the lines of "make a mod using the *Neverwinter Nights* engine." Several successful games have come out of successful mods, for example, *DOTA* and *PubG Battlegrounds*.
- One writer who applied to work for me had a PowerPoint pitch deck for a narrative game. You may never be asked to pitch a game, but a great pitch deck shows you understand how story and gameplay interact.
- Work in other media. I hired another writer partly because of a script she wrote for a comic. It showed she had a voice and a point of view. My own portfolio includes the opening from a TV pilot I developed for a network.

Things you were paid to write are better for your portfolios than stuff you made up. If it shipped, even better. Of course, you'll need to get permission from the rights owner.

If the game has not yet shipped and you can't get permission to use the material you wrote, then you can't legally use it. That's what that NDA (Non-Disclosure Agreement) you signed was about. However, I have heard *rumors* that *some* people remove anything that could identify what game their sample script came from and then put it in their portfolio. This is called "filing off the serial numbers," or so I am told.

In film and television, it does not occur to anyone to prevent you from using your paid work as a writing sample. Use your best judgment.

If you are submitting your portfolio to a company, consider whether it is the right portfolio for that company. First of all, read the specifications in the job posting. If they're asking for a comedy writing sample, make sure you send one in. You are not only showcasing your work, but you are also showcasing your ability to Read the Instructions.

If you're submitting to Larian (*Baldur's Gate*), you might want to show some conditional dialog. If you're submitting to Compulsion Games, which has so far never done a branching narrative, you may want more linear samples.

An epic fantasy sample might be appropriate for Bethesda, which made the epic fantasy adventure *Skyrim*, but if you were submitting to Dontnod, which makes the very contemporary and naturalistic *Life is Strange* series, it may not help. Kelsie Mhoon, Senior Narrative Designer at Obsidian:

> Want to write for action-oriented titles, like *Call of Duty* or *Overwatch?* Prioritize barks and snappy progression-focused cutscenes.
>
> Want to write for story-driven RPGs, like *Baldur's Gate 3* or *Disco Elysium?* Prioritize character voice, emotional story beats, and branching dialogue with player choice.
>
> … If you send in a full novel as a sample, that tells me you don't know your audience.[2]

Brooke Breit applied to *You Don't Know Jack*, the board game, with *You Don't Know Jack* questions:

> Writing trivia questions is one thing. But then, having that, "what's the premise, what's the spin, what's the joke?" There's multiple layers to writing a *You Don't Know Jack* question.[3]

And now she's Creative Director of Jackbox Games. (Caveat: sending a company a sample from their own i.p. is risky if you don't absolutely nail it. They are going to have a much narrower idea of what their game should sound like. The last thing you want is a reader going, "No, that's not really right.")

It's hard to stand out writing epic fantasy and space opera. Writing in other genres allows you to show that you know more than *Star Wars* and *Lord of the Rings*. I would not recommend including lore about a fantasy game world unless you can really bring something special to it.

Your samples need to get to the goods fast. If your first page doesn't grab them, they may not continue to the second. In fact, your first few lines had probably better grab them.

If you show someone your work, make sure it's your best work, the best you can do. If your stuff is not ready to be seen yet, wait until it is. As Eminem says, "You only get one shot, do not miss your chance to blow. This opportunity comes once in a lifetime, yo."

Okay, you probably will get more than one opportunity. But make sure you're ready for it. 80% of being lucky consists of putting yourself in the path of opportunity – and recognizing when there is an opportunity. You can't win the prize if you don't buy a ticket.

Make sure you *have* work to show. Someone told Lisa that she wanted to get into screenwriting. Lisa offered to read her stuff. She didn't have any stuff yet. Whoops. I told a TV writer I might have a game writing job they'd be right for in, oh, six months. When the job opened six months later, they still only had TV samples. Their game samples weren't ready. Whoops.

WEBSITE

A lot of writers have their own websites these days. It is super easy and cheap to make your own website. Google Sites allows you to buy your own domain (say, http://alexmakesstuffup.com) for, like, $20 a year and provides you with easy tools for formatting a simple site. Other sites like WordPress provide more powerful tools.

I'm up in the air about whether to include a link to a portfolio on your website. On one hand, it sure makes it easy for someone to see if you can write. On the other hand, you can't control who's looking at it, and you can't tailor the portfolio to them. I don't include my portfolio on my site; if someone wants to read some of my stuff, I put together a portfolio just for them.

On the *other* hand, if you only have a few samples, I guess there's little downside to putting them up in public. I know a senior game writer who regularly puts fresh samples up on his social media. Your mileage may vary.

CV/RESUME

(CVs are called resumes in the United States.)

A resume you send to a specific company or person should be tailored to that specific company or person and the specific job you're applying for. Yes, that means you tweak it every time you send it out.

What relevant experience do you have? Obviously, game jobs are key. But having experience writing in another media is as important as non-writing experience in game development. Anything that sets you apart from other applicants for a job is useful.

When I was recruited for my current job, at a company based in China, I had relevant experience as a Narrative Director, had shipped some games, and had a portfolio they liked, so I was qualified. But I also had written two books on screenwriting, one of which had been translated into Chinese. Turned out none of the other candidates had a book on screenwriting available in Chinese.

(It also did not hurt that I'd played D&D with one of the two guys interviewing me. *That's* how you get hired in the game industry.)

Knowing how to work in Unreal Engine is a plus when approaching companies that use it; knowing any game engine well is always a plus.

I know several game writers who started as game journalists. The difference between a small pizza and game journalism is that a small pizza will keep you from starving, but writing game journalism does give you the chance to meet creative people. A friend of mine did a series of interviews with developers from Harmonix, then got hired at Harmonix.

As a junior writer, you're likely going to write a lot of things that don't rely on game development knowledge. So having written a novel is a plus. Having done stand-up comedy is a plus. Having been a food writer is a plus. Having written radio commercials is a plus.

There is a person out there who offers resume-writing advice for a stiff fee. The style of resume that they recommend fronts skills rather than experience. It is the consensus of my senior video game writer friends that they do not want to see a resume listing your alleged skills. Employers want to see what jobs you've done.

I don't think your resume needs to say what job you're looking for. It's the job you just sent it in for, obviously.

Make sure your LinkedIn page functions as an alternate CV for you. Keep it updated and make sure it's clear.

A PERSONABLE LETTER

Your CV says what experiences you've had. Your cover email or uploaded cover letter is your chance to create a sense of yourself in a recruiter's or hiring manager's mind. You're a writer, right? Your cover letter should create a charismatic, likable *character* with the same name as you.

Your cover letter is the first bit of your writing they're going to see. It needs to *rock*.

That means no, don't use AI to write your cover letter. If you can't even write your own cover letter, why would we hire you?

Like your resume, your cover is tailored to the specific job you're applying for. Yes, that means you rewrite it every single time you apply to a job.

In fact, it is tailored to the *person* you are sending it to. Do your best to find out who that person is and send it directly to them. Don't be afraid to email or even call (gasp!) to find out who this person is.

If you don't have that person's email address, but the company has a standard protocol for email addresses, you can guess. For example, if you find one email address in the form cummerbund.bandersnatch@company.com, then it's a good bet that Bob Lastname's address is robert.lastname@company.com or bob.lastname@company.com. Or, if he's been there since the company was small, bob@company.com.

Don't recap your entire CV in the cover letter. A line or two quoting bits of the job listing, sure.

LinkedIn's job listings allow you to apply to jobs with a few clicks of a button. So many people apply through this feature to jobs for which they are hilariously unqualified, that employers may ignore the automatic applications. I certainly do.

KNOWLEDGE OF GAMES

This should be obvious, but you need to know games to write games. Ideally, you should *play* lots of games, but I know one or two writers and artists who just watch streamers play games.

You should play a lot of *different* games. I play a mix of AAA single-player adventure games and indie games. I play AAA games to know what the state of the art is – for example, what fully realized, fully voiced, well-acted, well-animated cinematics can and can't do.

I play indie games to see new things. Generally, if a lot of people on my social media are talking about a new game, I buy it and play it, too. Sometimes it's great, sometimes it's not, but it usually has something interesting worth talking about, and it's always important to know the games people talk about.

You do not need to play only games with strong narratives. I am a sucker for 4X games, sometimes known as "paint-the-map" games, where you start with a village or a county and take over the world. I have also played way too many hours of *Into the Breach*. Games with little narrative may give you ideas for how to integrate narrative into gameplay. They will also give you credibility as a gamer.

You do not have to finish all of these games. According to my Steam profile, I finish about one out of four of the games I start. In a few hours, you can usually see what the fuss is about. If it's a great story, play it through if you have the time. If it's not a great story, after about a dozen hours, you are mostly playing for fun.

Which, you know, is okay. Hopefully you're in the video game industry because you like to play video games.

FREE EXPERIENCE

You can get *some* experience in the industry by participating in game jams. These are super-short events where small teams get together to put together a rudimental version of a simple game in some insanely short period of time, like 48 hours.

Participating shows you're serious about working in the industry. You'll meet people who may become friends and contacts in the industry. And you can put your game jam experience on your CV.

WRITING TESTS

Some companies will ask you to do a writing test. Some of these have been exploitative: a week of unpaid work when you're one of dozens (or hundreds!) of people applying for the job. Some of these companies are starting to realize that this is not only exploitative and massively uncool, it's counter-productive. You don't want to restrict your applicant pool to people who have a spare week. People with jobs and kids, for example, do not have a spare week.

Some companies are willing to pay you to take their writing test. That's fairer, and encourages the company to test only those candidates it's serious about. It's also rare.

If you're doing a writing test, be sure to play enough of the company's games that you have a sense of the company's "voice," if they have one. You should be doing this any time you have an interview, too.

Katie Chironis's "donut volcano" Twitter thread from September 2020 would make a surprisingly acute writing test, and you could do worse than to be prepared for something like it:

> ONE: You're writing ability lines for a hero character in a pvp game. Her personality is "hot valkyrie with a katana." Write 20 lines for her, no more than 3 seconds each when spoken aloud or your audio director will hate you because she's chattering over gameplay.
>
> TWO: The player can unlock 20 different motorcycles. Name each motorcycle and write a lore blurb for it that is no longer than 80 words. The only thing that can visually change about the motorcycle is its color, the model is already locked and is identical for each motorcycle.
>
> THREE: Write a script for an NPC meant to help guide players through a tutorial. The NPC needs to be hilarious, not break the fourth wall, and also instruct the player on these subjects: how to fish, do a backflip, and change their graphics settings.
>
> FOUR: The NPC will ask the player to kill 40 forest wolves, 9 times. Write a short blurb that explains why this NPC needs the player to kill 450 forest wolves for some reason. Make it heartwarming, bleak, and memorable, but also keep in mind 98% of players won't read it.
>
> FIVE: We have a level. It's already fully complete with final art. It's an island with a volcano made out of literal donuts. Please write the intro VO a NPC will speak to the player which explains volcano donut island. No, it can't be funny. The game is extremely serious in tone.

GAME PROGRAMS

Hundreds of colleges and universities across the globe now offer either majors or classes in video game development. There are game writing classes in many creative writing programs as well.

Game design has become a common BFA or MFA program at art schools like NYU, USC, UCLA, SCAD, and Cal Arts, while universities like MIT and Carnegie Mellon offer video game writing classes.

Major programs for game writers and game developers include:

- USC
- NYU
- Savannah College of Art & Design (SCAD)
- Champlain College
- Clark University, MA
- Digipen Institute of Technology (Nintendo)
- Drexel University
- Michigan State
- Rensselaer Polytechnic
- Rochester
- University of Utah
- Vancouver Film School
- Worcester Polytechnic

Nobody *needs* a degree in games to get into games. A game program does give you something to put on your CV that shows you know a few basic things. It gives you time to focus on games without folks asking what are you doing with your life and when are you gonna get a job. And you can make friends who might help you later when *they* break into the industry.

WAR STORIES

People come into video game writing with a broad variety of qualifications, other than "rewrote a local hit movie" and "organized a panel discussion." Here are some examples:

- A young woman with experience as a substitute teacher went to game industry meetups and ended up chatting with a creative director. When he was hiring for a position as a video game editor, he called her. (You need a high charisma stat for this sort of thing.)

- A youngish person with no staff job experience wrote and programmed an indie game. So, when they applied for our job opening through LinkedIn, we knew they could write and had their own voice as a writer. Also, a game writer friend of theirs gave them a passionate recommendation.
- A young woman with no staff job experience but a successful Kickstarter for her comic came highly recommended by the person above.
- A senior writer friend of mine: "I was a tester at Activision on a mech game called *Mercenaries*, which I was really bad at, then I got into reviewing games for a magazine, where I was soon a columnist. Then some contacts at Activision hired me to write *Spider-Man 2* and it was all downhill from there."
- A young man with experience as a food writer came in with a recommendation from a writer on our staff, whose husband was his college roommate.
- A Narrative Director friend of mine started in showbiz like I did. Then "A friend of mine knew a game producer who wanted to make a 'Shooty, shooty alien bugs' type game and referred me. I got hired, but then because I was working at the studio then doing the marketing for *Starship Troopers*, there was some worry that people would think the game was ripping off the movie. So, I ended up writing the user manual of a samurai sword fighting game."
- A woman with a black belt in knife fighting and experience in stand-up comedy and writing radio commercials applied through regular channels.
- Another Narrative Director friend of mine: "I was hired to do an anime girl's field guide to New York, to be included with a *Sailor Moon* RPG adventure. I ended up being the company's office manager and contributing to various game books."
- An experienced woman writer I know: "I'd been doing branding for different companies and a lot of copywriting. And I was approached to help with media development on [AAA game]. The community developer's job was to create content based on the world of the game.

Everything from interviews with the developers and podcasts to in-character interviews and blogs."

- I met a young woman on the "Discord for Interactive Narrative" channel whose writing experience was writing magazines. She had some really impressive game writing samples on her personal web site.
- At least two current Narrative Directors I know got their start writing for tabletop role-playing games.
- A young woman we hired as a senior writer got her start in QA (Quality Assurance, aka testing). "I think it helped me understand the structure of a game. Also, I had to watch a scene multiple times.... So I quickly heard the difference between quippy fun dialogue, and dialogue that was uninspired or forced." She put together a portfolio of writing samples, and then was hired as a freelancer. That turned into her first permanent writing job.

F&*#$ YOU MONEY

If all goes well, at some point you will start earning more than enough to live on.

At that point, you want to start saving up "fuck you money." In any creative field, one of the best things about money is it enables you to say, "Fuck you, no" when you are offered an intolerable bargain. At least in your head. It might be an abusive situation at work. It might be a project that is creatively dead for you. It might be an insulting lowball job offer.

You don't get what you deserve. You get what you negotiate. It's hard to negotiate if you can't walk away.

Saving up is also critical because this is a cyclical industry. There are fat years and lean years. In lean years (like 2024 and 2008), there are lots of layoffs, and some people get shaken entirely out of the industry. You should never assume you'll have your job at the end of the year even if everyone likes your work. The game might get cut, your division might get cut. There may be politics you are unaware of. Think like a freelancer, not a salaried employee. You may have a good idea where your next paycheck is coming from, but you never really *know*.

"FAILURE IS NOT AN OPTION."

In creative fields, the standard advice is to stick it out no matter how bad it is. Keep at it, and your dream will come true. "Fail often; fail better," as Beckett said. The successful ones are the ones who never quit, no matter what.

And this is true – for those of us who made it. We got knocked down, we got back up again, over and over. There are almost no people who waltzed into a great job and then went on to success after success. Time wounds all heels.

But this is survivor bias.

There are also people who never quit, no matter what, who never made it. Some of them are as good as the ones that make it. The race is not always to the swift, nor battle to the strong. If you're not catching the breaks, if it seems impossible, absolutely you should ask yourself if you're barking up the wrong tree.

You are not a weak person if you decide, after getting kicked in the shins 1,000 times, that you've had it with getting kicked in the shins. It costs nothing to give earnest, optimistic advice, but they are your shins.

Consider whether there may be other things you could do that would make you feel happy and fulfilled.

Consider whether there may be other things you could *write* that would make you feel happy and fulfilled. From 1600 to 1850 or so, you could make a very good living as a poet. In 1950, you also had to teach. In 1950, you could make a good living as a playwright. In 2025, that's rare. In my time, TV writing and the music business have gone from fat years to lean years.

I was not terrifically successful as a film writer in LA. Sometimes you're just in the wrong market. So, I moved to Montreal. Did great as a Canadian TV writer. Then my little iceberg began to melt. Sometimes you're in the wrong epoch. So, I went into games.

And that's a *successful* trajectory.

I got married. Didn't work out. Second marriage is amazing. And *that's* a success story.

One of the worst relationships I ever had was after I did a life seminar based on the theory that you can make anything happen if you want it enough. Oh, my Lord, were we bad for each other! I don't think she even really *liked* me. But we stuck at it because we could make anything happen. Until we came to our senses. This notion of perseverance at all costs made us stick with a truly lousy relationship.

I knew a really terrific actress in LA. She had a transparent quality; her emotions just popped. She was a joy to work with. But it never happened for her. She quit to go into raising money for accessible playgrounds. That is awesome. I know another good actress who quit to become a pastry chef. That is also awesome.

Point is: if your plane is on fire, bail out. If your only legacy is the kind things you do for other people and the joy you took in sunsets and fresh bread, you will have lived a good life.

NOTES

1 I was once told, "You can be as difficult as you are talented." It has been my lifelong struggle to be as talented as I am difficult.

2 Kelsie Mhoon on Twitter, August 2, 2022, 1:13 PM.

3 Reality Escape Pod S8E4, https://www.podbean.com/ep/pb-f557d-171513f.

Appendix – Scene Checklist

Here are some questions to answer about a scene before you write it or even after you write it.

PRODUCTION QUESTIONS:

1. Why does this need to be a conversation? Conversations are expensive to realize, and they stop gameplay. Is there an in-game narrative delivery system that would do (scripted dialog event, audio flashback, readable, environmental narrative)?

NARRATIVE QUESTIONS

1. How does the main character feel coming into the scene? What happened earlier that day? What happened on the way in? Where are we physically?
2. How does the non-player character (NPC) feel coming into the scene? What does the PC want that the NPC doesn't want to give her?
3. Why doesn't the NPC want to give it to her?

    a. What is the PC doing and saying in order to get it that isn't simply asking for it? (E.g., shaming, guilting, offering a deal)

    b. Does she get it? What changes for her in the scene?

    c. How does she feel coming out of the scene?

4. What does the NPC want that the PC doesn't want to give them?

    a. Why doesn't the PC want to give it to them?

    b. What are they doing and saying to get it that isn't simply asking for it?

    c. What changes for them in the scene?

    d. How do they feel coming out of the scene?

5. What does this scene reveal about the PC?

6. What does it reveal about the NPC?

Extra Credit Narrative (makes a scene richer and more fun)

1. What happens in the scene that we did not expect?

2. What grounds this scene? What is the moment where we see ourselves, or people we know, in the scene?

3. What propels us out of the scene? (The "button.")

Animation Questions

1. What is the tone of the scene? (Foreboding, bittersweet, funny)

2. What is the "poster" for this scene? What single moment from the scene sums it all up?

3. Are there symbolic props or scenery?

4. What can we convey about the characters through staging and "acting" rather than dialog?

5. What happens in the moment of revelation or change?

Glossary

Here are my definitions of some game terms. Different companies may use the terms differently.

Aria: When a character goes on at length about something emotional. Arias can be brilliant. They can reveal character; they can make us care. Arias had better be brilliant, because they stop the story dead.

Artifact: Something left over from a previous draft that no longer makes sense or serves its purpose. Narrative cruft.

Asset: A single object that exists in the game, such as a gun, a tree, and a beer can. An asset can be easily cloned. Environmental artists make assets. Narrative folk may write text for assets that have labels. What's on the labels of beer cans in this world?

As You Know, Bob: Dialog that recounts what both characters in the scene already know, so the player can know it, too. If you must deliver exposition, at least have them argue.

Bible: A compendium of all the information developers once thought they needed to make the game. Out of date moments after it is written, or purely aspirational from the get-go. Usually assigned to the least experienced member of the team, with the consequences you'd expect. The "narrative bible" might have information about the *world story* as well as the characters' backstories. Once production begins, developers tend to stop updating the bible, so double-check any information you read in it by talking to the narrative team.

It's helpful if writing a bible to focus on things that can actually appear in the game rather than Tolkien-style lore about the battle for Morgoliath in the Second Age. Also, remember that a bible is not player-facing. Narrative you write in the bible is not in the game until or unless you, or a level artist, put it in the game using a narrative delivery system.

Break Story: Laying the story down beat by beat, ideally in a room (or a virtual room) full of writers. Ironically, when you "break" story, you are actually building it; often there was no story there before, only a premise and an ending. Look, I don't make the rules.

Bump: Something that bothers you about a story and throws you out of immersion. "Goddamn it, parsecs are a measure of distance, not time!" "*That's* what you're bumping on???"

Button: A punchy way to end a scene, providing the energy to jump back into gameplay. "Needs a button."

Cinematic: A short movie that interrupts gameplay. Level designers often hate them. May be pre-rendered, in which case it really is a movie playing in the middle of the game. Or it may be animated via the game engine using the character models and environments of the game. Some studios use "cutscene" to distinguish in-engine cinematics from rendered cinematics, but the distinction is not universal.

Clam: An overused phrase or gimmick. "He's standing right behind me, isn't he?" "Wait, I can explain!" "Did I just say that out loud?" "My work here is done."

Consumables: Anything the player character can use up, such as health potions, grenades, or food. Usually found in the environment or bought in stores in-game. If you find yourself in a large room with health potions and ammo scattered around, expect a boss battle.

Couplet: Two lines, usually brief, one answering the other. Often used to button a scene. "I'm a man!" "Nobody's perfect." TV Showrunner John Rogers calls this "the basic molecule of script dialogue."

Dependencies: Ways in which narrative delivery systems interact with other disciplines. Readables, for example, have almost no dependencies. They are assets that can be strewn about the environment by the most junior of level designers or even a writer. (Gasp.) If they convey lore about the world, they don't affect the game's story. By contrast, a cinematic has lots of dependencies. It can't be written until we know what the story is. It will require animation and possibly motion capture. An actor has to record lines, which have to be mixed. Etc.

Deus Ex Machina: Literally "God out of the machine." An event, usually towards the end of the story, that the player character did not cause to happen, and that neatly resolves their problems.

Downloadable Content (DLC): Additional content for the game. May have new maps and tell a completely new story. "DLC" is also what your producer promises you when they cut the levels you've been working on for a year.

Encounter: What happens when the player character runs into someone or something. Level designers create and script encounters. If it's a dialog encounter, narrative folks will write the dialog, Lord willing.

Environmental Artist: An artist who creates assets that will appear in the game. They may put them in the game map, if they don't affect gameplay; level designers may put them in the map if they do.

(The game map, in this sense of the word, is the collection of assets in the computer that create a level, that is, a section of the game world that you can move through seamlessly. You can open up the map in a game engine like Unreal Engine and fly through it.)

Narrative folk work with artists to make sure the environment tells the world story. For example:

> This was once a grand palace, but now it is covered in weeds. Sprawled here and there on the floors and benches, servants, courtiers, knights, and ladies sleep dreamlessly.

Environmental Narrative: Narrative descriptions of the game environment, creating a world story, a mystery, a mood, or anything else that attracts us to play in this world and makes us care. Each major location in a game might have its own narrative description, in addition to whatever notes the art director is giving her artists.

Environmental Scenario: A few items laid out in the environment to tell a story. For example,

> A table covered with playing cards. Two chairs, one fallen backwards. Dried blood spattered on the cards. A bottle shattered by a bullet. Under the table, a scrap of paper – on interacting with it, it turns out to be an IOU.

Narrative folk write these descriptions to convey the *world story*. Ideally, an environmental scenario uses assets that already exist, or are already planned for the game. Creating a single asset for an environmental scenario can take an artist a week, which is expensive. The sooner you can get these to the environmental artists, the better.

The difference between an environmental scenario and an environmental narrative is just scope. A scenario is a single collection of assets intended to convey a single idea. Environmental narrative encompasses everything that conveys what the world is.

Exotic: Something that only happens once or twice in the game or in only one level. Exotic gameplay might be when a level introduces tightrope-walking as a verb, but there are no tightropes to walk on later on in the game.

Filing Off the Serial Numbers: Suppose your best and most recent work is a cinematic script that you're not allowed to show due to an NDA (see below). What do you use in your portfolio? Sometimes, the answer is a cinematic script with very similar dialog, but different character and place names, and nothing that would identify the game you wrote it for. The serial numbers have been filed off, see?

I don't do that, but I've shipped a bunch of games. When you're starting out, proprietary work may be the only work you can show.

If you have work in your portfolio with serial numbers filed off, maybe don't post your portfolio in public on your website. Just send that material to people who ask to see your stuff.

First Person: A way of showing the player the world in three dimensions as if through the player character's eyes. The player character is usually invisible, though sometimes you can see your hands. First-person games are more likely to have a blank main character, so the player feels like it is them in the game world.

First-Person Shooter, or FPS: A first-person 3D game in which you shoot people in the face.

FrieNDA: Game writers are usually forbidden from talking about their projects to anyone outside the company; we have to sign an NDA, or "Non-Disclosure Agreement." Since we are human beings and need advice from peers, we do anyway. When you show your friend your work secretly, you are said to be operating under "FrieNDA," meaning, "I'm telling you this, but for the love of Pete don't tell anyone else."

Fridge Logic: A logic problem in your story that no one is going to notice until they get up and go to the fridge. Often not worth fixing. "C'mon, that's fridge logic."

Gameplay Designer: Someone who designs gameplay *features*, such as verbs. A gameplay mechanic that works on most of the game's levels is a feature.

Gray Box: An early state of a level, before the environmental art is in. Looks like a bunch of gray boxes. No point arting up a level before you know if it works.

Hang a Lantern on It: To draw attention to something. If there's something you really want the player to know, you hang a lantern on it somehow.

You can sometimes get away with inconsistencies by hanging a lantern on them. In *We Happy Few,* for gameplay reasons, Arthur could go into Sally's place via the back door, but, for level design reasons, we couldn't allow Sally to go out in her playthrough. So, we had her say, "Damn door. Always jamming." So long as the players know that *you* know it's inconsistent, they are more likely to forgive you than if they think that you're being sloppy or that you think they're too stupid to notice. They know it's a game, eh?

Hat on a Hat: Gilding the lily. Trying to make something stronger or funnier by adding something else strong or funny, thereby weakening it. A hat does not need a hat on it. A man in a gorilla suit is funny. Give him a clown nose as well, and you have a hat on a hat.

Hero's Journey: A sequence of tropes that appear in many mythical hero stories, according to Joseph Campbell. Often misused as a step-by-step prescription for the plot. Actual mythical hero stories rarely have all the steps, many of the steps are vague as hell, no one wants a predictable plot, and some steps don't work for games at all. But non-writers like it because they can ask, "But how does this line up with the Hero's Journey?" and feel they are on top of things.

Idiot Ball: When a character makes an out-of-character and obviously dumb decision, they are carrying the idiot ball.

Interlocutor: A fancy term for someone who's in the story for the main character to talk to. When you have a stoic, laconic character, we often give them a talkative sidekick who can ask the questions the laconic character isn't talking about.

Kill Your Darlings: A darling is a bit of narrative you particularly like and are particularly proud of – but it isn't actually good for the story as a whole.

Laying Pipe: Setting something up early that will pay off later. Akin to installing pipes so you can use the sink later.

Level: A hunk of the game map that is loaded into the consoles or computer's memory at one time. In Unreal Engine, a level is usually on a single *map*. Levels may or may not be apparent to the player. If levels are separated by *loading screens*, they will be pretty obvious, but next-generation consoles don't necessarily need loading screens. Depending on the size of the team, a single level designer may "own" or be responsible for a level.

Level Designer: Someone who designs the levels and what happens in them. Their job is to make gameplay fun. They have to know how the features of the game – especially the *verbs* – can work together. Often have a god complex. They create worlds, after all.

Loading Screen: What you see on the screen while the console or computer is putting the next level in memory. Usually, a still image with some text, or a simple, repetitive animation. Can be used to remind the player what's happened so far in the game, or to reveal some aspect of the world story, or to give gameplay hints. The loading screens for *Spec Ops: The Line* mock the player, "Do you feel like a hero yet?"

Magic Hat: A Magic Hat is a special power that you don't explain because the explanation wouldn't actually resolve anything. The point of magic is that it's magic. You can create lore behind a magic hat (e.g., the One Ring, Excalibur). What you don't need is a scientific explanation:

> Midi-chlorians were intelligent microscopic life forms that lived symbiotically inside the cells of all living things. In sufficient numbers, they could allow their symbiont to detect the pervasive energy field known as the Force. Midi-chlorian counts were blah bitty blah blah blah.

And what gives midi-chlorians this power? Their magic hats? You're just kicking the can down the road.

Moishe the Explainer: A character who exists primarily to give exposition to the player. Doesn't want anything from the player character, just wants to give them information. In *Austin Powers*, his name is Basil Exposition.

Narrative Designer: Someone on the narrative team who focuses on getting the content *into* the game rather than creating the content. They might place assets into the level map. They might do some scripting. They work with the level designers to make sure that the gameplay is, as much as possible, also telling the story of the main character and of the world.

A narrative systems designer defines narrative delivery systems for the game. In a smaller team, that job might be folded into narrative design, or even writing.

The dividing line between writers and narrative designers is blurry. Some narrative designers write player-facing narrative content. Others don't. Some writers do narrative design, whether they call it that or not. I've never had a job with "narrative design" in the title, but I've done a lot of narrative design.

NDA: A Non-Disclosure Agreement. A legal document you generally have to sign before you even interview at a company, saying that they can sue you if you reveal anything about their projects or your work that is not already known to the public. (See FrieNDA and "filing off the serial numbers" above.) Show business projects almost never have them, but for historical reasons, game companies are terrified that people will find out what they're working on. There have been enough Twitter mobs based on leaks that they're not entirely wrong.

Platformer: A game focused on how the player character gets from point A to point B.

Player-facing: Something players will experience in the game. Lore is not player-facing until it appears in narrative delivery system such as a *readable*, a *journal entry*, or an environmental asset such as tavern sign.

Quest Giver: Anyone who gives the player character a mission, but often someone who has nothing better to do than stand by the side of the road waiting to give the player character a quest.

Readable: An asset that exists to be read. Often when you interact with it, you can read some text on a separate screen, for example as an entry in the player's journal or inventory. A poster for shaving lotion that you can read as you ride into town is not considered a readable. It's a "decal" – a texture that you can slap onto a surface in the game world. Readables are by far the cheapest way to get lore into the game.

Most developers will not put anything critical into a readable, since God forbid the player should have to read something. (What is this, a *library?*) *Baldur's Gate 3* bravely puts critical information in readables. That's a game design decision, not a narrative decision.

Reset the Sign: The sign is, "It has been X days since someone mentioned The Hero's Journey," the trope pattern that is the bane of all the writers I know. When someone mentions it, it's time to reset the sign back to 0.

Run and Jump: Describes a section of traversal in a game. "And here we have a little run and jump until we get into our first combat encounter."

Scope: How big the game is and how much work it's going to be. Narrative scope is how much narrative the team will have to create. Games start with big ambitions and, over time, have to be slimmed down.

Scope Creep: The tendency for the scope of a game to get bigger as people come up with great ideas. Not a bad thing in itself, but someone's gonna have to pay for it.

Second Draft: Something meaningful in screenwriting contracts and which producers like to put in their narrative pipeline chart. It's not really a thing. Writers may write a vomit draft, a rough draft, and a first draft. You may get your draft approved and eventually recorded. But all the drafts between the first draft and the approved draft – why count them? How many changes do you need to make for it to be a second draft? Every draft should be considered a first draft until it's recorded.

Shmup: A shoot'em up. A *shooter.* As opposed to a beat'em-up, a game focused on melee combat.

Shoe Leather: The narrative hoops you have to jump through to set something up dramatically – e.g., establish that the hero is an orphan, remind the audience of their psychokinetic abilities, etc. all so it pays off later. Not that far off from laying pipe, but more of a criticism. "That's all just shoe leather."

Shooter: Any game focused on shooting NPCs. Game developers add "in the face" almost instinctively.

Snappy Banter: As a putdown, dialog that sounds clever and punchy but has little emotional content.

Table Read: A readthrough of all the dialog scenes. On the first day of rehearsals for a play, the playwright, director, and all the actors would get together and read the play, sitting down. Our version might be on Zoom, to make it easier to get actors to participate. Pay the actors if you possibly can. *You're* getting paid, aren't you?

Taking the Curse Off: When something is cliché or dumb, you may not be able to get rid of it for reasons. But you can sometimes take the curse off it by twisting it in some way.

Telegraphing: Foreshadowing. Giving the players too heavy a hint where the story will go. You don't want to telegraph the punchline to a joke. Comes from sending a telegraph saying you're coming, rather than just showing up.

Traversal: Gameplay focused on getting from here to there. Narrative audio is traditionally constrained by the assumption that the player will traverse the level as fast as the game allows them, even though most players may not. If the narrative is longer than the minimum traversal time, you need a game mechanic to prevent narrative audio from stacking up.

TV Tropes: A compendium of familiar tropes and how they are used in various media, including TV, film, and games. It is fascinating, fun, and a huge rabbit hole. I rarely get off that site in less than an hour. I warned you.

Twitch: A streaming platform, but also gameplay where success depends on quick reflexes. I am not good at twitch games.

Unobtainium: The substance that everybody in the game world wants but is hard to get. It might be the thing you need to make the best sword or a spaceship. In *Avatar*, it is literally called unobtainium. Common in fantasy (mithril) as well as science fiction (dilithium crystals, "red matter," motilene, radianite, glunite).

Up and Back: When the characters or plot go through action sequences, dialog scenes, complications, etc., but the story does not progress. You can cut out an up and back, and you won't feel anything is missing.

Verb: Any action the player can take in the gameplay, for example, "walk," "jump," or "dodge." A *shooter* has specialized verbs like "shoot," "take cover" (if it's a cover shooter), "stealth takedown" (if stealth is a mechanic), and "throw" (if you can throw grenades or other consumables.) A platformer might have verbs like "climb," "mantle" and "use zipline." A walking simulator might have "examine."

The first question I ask about a game idea is, "what are the verbs?"

Walking Simulator: Originally a dismissive joke, but now a legit genre. A game in which you walk around and look at things. *Gone Home* is the type specimen for the current iteration of the genre. You just walk around a house, read some stuff, look at some stuff, and solve some not very hard puzzles in order to open up more parts of the house and learn what became of your missing sister.

In a walking simulator, there is no combat, or trivial combat, and traversal is not particularly hard. It's all about the environmental narrative and the audio.

WNF: "Will Not Fix." Towards the end of a game's production, QA writes flocks of bug reports. If something is too hard or too trivial to fix, developers respond with "WNF." It may also be something QA thinks is a bug, but is fact the intended design.

World Story: The history of the world, as distinct from what happens during the game. What sort of world we're in can be as, or more, important than the player character story. There may be a *bible* that defines the world story. It is already hilariously out of date.

Writer: A person with a socially acceptable and sometimes paying addiction. Often seen at parties hanging out with the ferns.

There is no known cure.

A Random Assortment of Games to Play

Here are some games you might want to be able to talk about, either because they are interesting and obscure and you will score points for knowing about them, or because everyone mentions them.

These are also good games to tell people about who are intrigued by games, but who don't want to shoot or punch people in the face.

This is a list skewed toward narrative, not too difficult games, and games available on both Mac and PC games.

Mac/PC – small non-twitch games

- *80 Days*: Based on the novel by Jules Verne, if Europe didn't colonize the world.
- *West of Loathing*: Really silly and adorable side-scrolling stick-figure Western.
- *Return of the Obra Dinn*: Puzzle game in which you must figure out how the 60 people on the Obra Dinn died, and therein lies a sea story.
- *Black Book*: Deckbuilder about a Slavic witch on a very dubious quest.
- *Passage*: The most primitive imaginable side-scroller which, notwithstanding may make you weep.
- *Inscryption*: A psychological horror escape-room deckbuilder.
- *Unpacking*: A weirdly moving game in which you move into a series of new places to live. Seriously, though.
- *Papo & Yo*: A parable.

- *Gorogoa*: A sort of puzzle game where a story unfolds as you move pictures around.
- *Baba Is You*: A word puzzle game. Gets difficult eventually, but you can stop any time.

Mac/PC – bigger games – casual gameplay

- *Disco Elysium* – A decayed detective trying to solve a murder gets caught up in the politics of an equally decayed Empire.
- *Contrast*: You are the circus girl who is the invisible friend of Didi, an 8-year-old trying to uncover the secrets of her past. You can become your own shadow, and walk on shadows.
- Stray: You are a cat, trying to escape a city of robots. Fantastic environmental narrative.

Mac/PC – games where you have to hack and slash a bit

- *Cult of the Lamb*: You are a lamb trying to bring back a bloodthirsty elder god.
- *Boyfriend Dungeon*: Date your swords.
- *We Happy Few*: Three slightly horrible people try to escape an insane, groovy dystopian England.
- *Banner Saga*: Vikings and killer robots from space. Turn-based tactical combat, meaning that you can take as long as you like.
- *Into the Breach*: Fight giant bugs with mechs. Totally addictive turn-based tactical. A gem of its kind.
- *Subnautica*: Offworld survival game with a deep backstory you discover by plunging ever deeper.

PC only – small

- *What Remains of Edith Finch*: What happened to the Finch family in this creepy old house?

- *Journey*: A mysterious character tries to get to the top of that mountain. Creates a mood without saying a word.
- *Papers, Please*: A depressing and powerful game about being a bureaucrat in a vaguely Eastern European dictatorship.
- *The Stanley Parable*: An iconic game about choices that is also a parody of games about choices.
- *Where the Water Tastes Like Wine*: How folk tales grow.

Legit big games

- *Baldur's Gate 3*: 2023's breakout narrative game. The gold standard for a narrative game with conditional dialog, where choices matter.
- *Hades*: Roguelike with an unfathomably deep well of dialog and a very satisfying game loop tied into it.
- *The Last of Us*: Strong story, strong characters, good dialog, convincing realization. Overused as an example. Bear in mind, it is a *very* traditional, linear narrative experience, with cinematics punctuating stretches of gameplay.

Index

Made in the USA
Las Vegas, NV
30 March 2026

44471744R10111